pavlov conditioned voca

파블로프 영단어

저자 **한희영**

파블로프 영단어

발행일   2022년 7월 25일

지은이   한희영
펴낸이   손형국
펴낸곳   (주)북랩
편집인   선일영   편집   정두철, 배진용, 김현아, 박준, 장하영
디자인   이현수, 김민하, 김영주, 안유경   제작   박기성, 황동현, 구성우, 권태련
마케팅   김회란, 박진관
출판등록 2004. 12. 1(제2012-000051호)
주소   서울특별시 금천구 가산디지털 1로 168, 우림라이온스밸리 B동 B113~114호, C동 B101호
홈페이지 www.book.co.kr
전화번호 (02)2026-5777   팩스   (02)2026-5747

ISBN   979-11-6836-422-6 13740 (종이책)   979-11-6836-423-3 15740 (전자책)

(주)북랩 성공출판의 파트너
북랩 홈페이지와 패밀리 사이트에서 다양한 출판 솔루션을 만나 보세요!
홈페이지 book.co.kr   •   **블로그** blog.naver.com/essaybook   •   **출판문의** book@book.co.kr

작가 연락처 문의 ▶ ask.book.co.kr
작가 연락처는 개인정보이므로 북랩에서 알려드릴 수 없습니다.

파블로프의 개처럼
영단어가 떠오른다

심리학과 영단어 학습의
환상적 컬래버레이션

Tutorial

가볍게 읽고
학습을 시작하세요!

파블로프 영단어
Tutorial

다음에 나열된 영단어들의 뜻을 적어 주세요. 아주 쉬운 수준의 단어는 아닙니다.
※ 만약 영단어를 보고 그 뜻이 바로 떠오르지 않는다면, 고민하지 말고
   꼭 오른쪽 페이지를 참고하여 뜻을 적어 주세요!
※ 똑같은 단어가 무작위로 반복해서 나옵니다. 같은 단어가 두 번 세 번 나오
   더라도 뜻이 바로 떠오르지 않으면, 오른쪽 페이지의 뜻을 보고 적으면 됩니다.

recidivism	baleful
baleful	ineluctable
incumbent	importune
importune	recidivism
devout	importune
ineluctable	baleful
recidivism	devout
ineluctable	incumbent
incumbent	ineluctable
baleful	recidivism
devout	devout
importune	importune
recidivism	ineluctable
incumbent	baleful
devout	incumbent

recidivism	상습적 범행, 재범
importune	성가시게 조르다
ineluctable	불가피한, 피할 수 없는
devout	독실한
incumbent	재임 중인
baleful	악의적인, 해로운

첫 페이지부터 단어를 제시하고 사전 암기도 없이 바로 뜻을 써 보라고 해서 조금 당황하셨죠? 물론 영단어를 먼저 암기한 후 테스트에 들어간다면, 학습 결과는 더 좋을 수 있습니다. 하지만 『파블로프 영단어』에서는 이 과정을 과감히 생략하였습니다. 그 이유는 차근차근 설명하겠습니다.

무엇인가에 대해 아는지 모르는지 스스로 조절하는 능력을 '메타 인지'라고 합니다. 다음은 메타 인지와 관련한 강의의 내용을 간추린 것입니다.

> **"여러분에게 대한민국의 수도를 아느냐고 물어보면,**
> **여러분은 주저 없이 '네'라고 말할 것입니다.**
> **하지만 여러분에게 과테말라에서 세 번째로 큰 도시를 아느냐고 물어보면,**
> **'아니오'라는 대답이 먼저 나올 것입니다."**
>
> tvN 〈어쩌다 어른〉 中에서

메타 인지가 무엇인지 아주 쉽게 이해되시죠?

이러한 메타 인지 능력은 인간만이 가진 특별한 능력입니다. 컴퓨터는 파일을 전체 스캔한 후 결과를 말해 주지만. 인간은 뇌를 전체 스캔하지 않고 바로 대답이 나옵니다. 이것은 인간만이 가지고 있는 특별한 능력이기도 합니다.

또 한 가지 예를 들어 볼까요?

> **"자동차가 고장 나면 우리는 보닛을 열어 봅니다.**
> **사실 보닛을 열어도 아무것도 할 수 없는 우리지만, 일단 열어 보게 되죠?**
> **자동차가 익숙하므로, 자동차의 구조도 잘 알 것이라고 착각하기 때문입니다."**
>
> tvN 〈어쩌다 어른〉 中에서

이처럼 메타 인지 능력에 대해 쉽게 예를 들어 표현했는데요. 다시 말해 메타 인지란 인지적 활동에 대한 지식과 조절을 의미합니다. 더 쉽게 표현하면 부족한 부분을 채우기 위해, 나의 학습을 평가하며 보완하는 과정을 말합니다.

모든 인간은 이와 같은 메타 인지 능력을 가지고 있습니다. 인간이 가지고 있는 방대한 지식의 양을 고려했을 때, 내가 모르는 것에 대해서만큼은, 그 어떤 슈퍼컴퓨터도 따라올 수 없을 정도로 빠른 판단 능력을 갖추고 있죠. 그러나 이 메타 인지 능력은 익숙한 것이 나타나기 시작하면, 얼마나 잘 알고 있는지에 대해서 착각을 하기 시작합니다. 익숙한 것과 아는 것, 그 모호한 경계에 대해 심리학자들은 이렇게 말합니다.

"세상에는 두 가지 종류의 지식이 있습니다. 첫 번째는 내가 알고 있다는 느낌은 있는데 설명할 수 없는 지식이고, 두 번째는 내가 알고 있다는 느낌뿐만 아니라 남들에게 설명할 수도 있는 지식입니다. 두 번째 지식만이 진짜 지식이며, 쓸모 있는 지식입니다."

메타 인지적 관점에서 인지는, 세 단계로 나눌 수 있습니다

1 ○	2 ◐	3 ●
모르는 것	알고 있는 느낌은 들지만 설명할 수 없는 것	알고 있다는 느낌뿐만 아니라 설명할 수도 있는 것

알고 있다는 느낌과 모른다는 느낌은 구분을 잘하지만, 내가 알고 있다는 느낌이 드는 (익숙한 것과 아는 것) 지식은 구분이 어렵다는 내용인데요. 그렇다면 이 구분은 어떻게 할까요? 이는 바로 끊임없는 테스트를 통해 구분할 수 있습니다. 즉, 익숙한 것을 지식으로 착각하고 있지는 않은지 말이죠. 우리가 시험장에서나 실생활에서 영어 단어를 접할 때, 가끔 이런 경우가 있습니다.

"분명 아는 단어인데, 갑자기 뜻이 기억이 나질 않네?"
이처럼 분명히 봤고 알던 단어인데, 전혀 뜻이 생각나지 않을 때를 메타 인지적 관점으로 보게 되면, 이런 경우는 익숙한 단어일 뿐, 지식으로 평가받을 수 없는 경우라고 말할 수 있습니다. 우리가 아는 단어라면 당연히 뜻을 쓰거나 설명할 수 있어야 합니다. 갑자기 기억이 안 나는 경우는 없다는 뜻이죠!

테스트에서 높은 점수를 받기 위해서는 암기 과정을 따로 두는 것보다, 잦은 테스트를 통해 암기하는 것이 효과적입니다. 테스트를 통해 암기하는 것은 우리가 실제 지식과 익숙한 단어를 구분해서 외울 수 있는 좋은 방법이죠.

**이런 이유로 『파블로프 영단어』에서는
암기보다는 테스트에 중점을 두었습니다.**

완벽한 암기 없이 시험을 본다는 게 다소 이해가 안 될 수도 있지만, 진행하시다 보면 무턱대고 외우는 것보다 암기에 효과가 있다는 걸 느끼시게 될 겁니다.

학습에 있어 메타 인지적 학습도 중요하지만, 또 하나 중요한 것이 있습니다. 바로 영단어를 보고, 뜻을 떠올릴 때까지 걸리는 시간인데요. 야박하다고 느끼실 수 있지만 영단어를 보고 뜻을 설명하거나 쓸 수 있더라도, 영단어의 뜻을 판단하는 시간이 길어서도 안 됩니다. 즉, 영단어를 보았을 때 0.5초 이내로 뜻이 떠올라야 합니다.

조건화

왜 0.5초 이내여야만 하는지 설명하기에 앞서 우선 조건화에 대해 알아야 하는데요. 조건화란 아무 의미 없는 자극(조건)과 특정 반응을 연관 지어 의미 있는 자극으로 만드는 것입니다. 정리하자면, 특정 자극을 주면 특정 반응을 보이게 만드는 것은 조건화라고 말하고, 조건화가 된다면 우리는 '조건 반사' 한다고 말합니다.

영단어 학습은 알고 보면 조건화하는 과정입니다. 영어 단어라는 특정 자극을 접했을 때, '우리말 뜻'이라는 특정한 반응을 나올 수 있도록 하는 건데요. 'book'이란 단어를 듣거나 봤을 때(특정 자극을 접했을 때), 우리말인 '책'이라는 뜻이 바로 튀어나올 수 있게 학습하는 거죠. 더 깊게 보자면 우리말 뜻인 '책'보다 우리가 생각하는 '책의 이미지'를 반사적으로 튀어나오게 하는 것이 영어 학습의 목표입니다.

| 그림 1. 무조건 반사

목줄을 한 강아지 가까이에 먹이를 놓아두었더니 강아지가 침을 흘렸다.

| 그림 2. 무반응

목줄을 한 강아지에게 종소리를 들려주었더니 아무 반응이 없었다.

| 그림 3. 조건화 학습

목줄을 한 강아지에게 종소리를 들려준 후 먹이 주는 것을 반복했다.

| 그림 4. 조건 반사

목줄을 한 강아지는 어느새 종만 쳐도 침을 흘렸다.

위의 실험은 유명한 '조건화' 실험입니다. 어려운 말로 '고전적 조건화'에 관한 실험인데요. 여기서부턴 '고전적'이라는 말을 빼고 '조건화'라고 줄여 말하겠습니다.

① 목줄을 한 강아지 가까이에 먹이를 놓아두었더니 강아지가 침을 흘렸다(무조건 반사).

먹이가 가까이 있으면, 침을 흘리는 것은 조건 반사가 아닙니다. 조건 반사는 앞서 말했다시피 조건화가 된 이후에 반응하는 것을 조건 반사라고 합니다. 먹이를 보면 침을 흘리는 것은 동물이 태어날 때부터 가지고 있는 반응으로, 조건화가 필요 없는 반응이라 하여 무조건 반사라고 합니다. 그리고 여기서 먹이는 무조건 반사를 일으키는 무조건자극이죠.

② 목줄을 한 강아지에게 종소리를 들려주었더니 아무 반응이 없었다(무반응).

목줄을 한 강아지에게 종소리를 들려주었더니 강아지의 침샘에서 아무런 반응이 없었습니다. 이것은 아직 조건화되지 않았기 때문이죠. 그래서 우리는 여기서 종소리를 중립 자극이라고 합니다.

③ 목줄을 한 강아지에게 종소리를 들려준 후 먹이 주는 것을 반복했다(조건화 학습).

파블로프는 강아지의 침샘을 다루는 다른 연구에서, 강아지가 먹이를 들고 있는 사육사의 발걸음소리만 들어도 침을 흘린다는 사실을 발견하고, 종소리를 들리게 한 후 먹이 주는 것을 반복하였습니다. 이를 조건 형성이라고 하는데요. 조건화를 위한 학습이죠.

④ 목줄을 한 강아지는 어느새 종만 쳐도 침을 흘렸다(조건 반사).

③의 조건 형성 학습을 반복하였더니, 어느덧 강아지가 종소리만 들려도 침을 흘리며 조건화 되었습니다.

조건화에 대해 이해가 되셨나요? 여기까지가 유명한 '파블로프의 실험'인데요.

하나의 자극과 빠르게 연이어 또 다른 자극을 짝지어 주는 것을 반복하면, 조건화되어 반응하는 것이죠.

판단의 시간 0.5초

0.5초는 이해가 아닌 단순 암기에서, 학습 시간의 최소 단위입니다. 학습심리학 연구가 세바스티안 라이트너(1919-1989)는 저서 『공부의 비결』에서 "0.5초는 행동과 사고의 기준이 되는 최소 시간"이며, **"0.5초는 모든 인생의 중심축"**이라고 말합니다.

라이트너는 그의 저서에서 사무라이의 노스승들이 제자가 우물 위로 허리를 굽힐 때나 말에 먹이를 줄 때, 또는 낙엽을 긁어모을 때, 시도 때도 없이 갑자기 나타나 대나무 막대기로 제자의 머리를 내리치는 것뿐만 아니라, 미국 서부의 총잡이들이 최대한 빠르게 '총 뽑기' 연습을 하는 것 역시도 0.5초 안에 반응하기 위한 이유라고 주장했습니다. 정확히 말하자면 '조건화'를 위한 훈련은 0.5초의 시간 간격이 중요하다는 것이죠.

자동차 운전자가 장애물을 만나 상황 판단 후, 브레이크를 밟는 데 걸리는 반응 시간도 0.5초입니다. 그러므로 단어를 보고 0.5초 내에 영단어의 뜻을 설명하거나, 글로 쓸 수 없다면 조건화되지 않은 것입니다.

0.5초 만에 판단되지 않는다면, 재차 조건화 훈련을 해야 합니다.

---

car run love angry winter beautiful

위 단어들을 보면, 몇 초 이내에 뜻이 떠오르시나요? 0.5초? 아마 0.5초보다 더 빠르게 반응하셨을 것입니다. 오랜 시간 동안 우리에게 노출되어 훌륭하게 조건화된 단어들이지요. 그렇다면 조건화 훈련은 어떻게 해야 할까요?

● 단어 학습에서 '조건'화

특히, 단어 학습과 같은 단순 학습은 조건화 학습의 정점입니다. 모국어뿐만 아니라 모든 단어와 관련된 학습은 조건화 학습입니다. 우리는 단어를 결코 서술적인 기억으로 저장해 놓지 않습니다.

'축구'라는 단어를 들었을 때 우리는 '운동장에서 사람들과 가죽으로 된 공을 발로 차면서, 양쪽으로 공격 또는 수비하고, 공이 득점 라인을 넘어가면 득점으로 인정하는 구기 스포츠 중 하나'라고 생각하지 않습니다. 대화 중, '축구'라는 단어가 나왔을 때 그렇게 생각할 겨를도 없고요.

심지어 위에 예를 든 '운동장, 사람, 가죽, 공, 발, 공격, 수비, 득점' 등 단어 역시 서술적인 기억으로 회상해 낸다면 '축구'라는 단어 하나를 들었을 때, 뜻을 유추해 내는 시간도 3~4분 이상 걸릴 것입니다.

● 영단어 '조건'화

이제부터 우리는 영단어를 '조건'으로 간주합니다. 영단어의 뜻이 떠오르기 위한 '조건'인 것이죠. 즉, 파블로프의 실험에서 볼 수 있었던 '종'과 같은 역할입니다. 그리고 영단어의 우리말 뜻은 '반사(반응)'입니다. 마찬가지로 파블로프의 실험에서 '강아지의 침'과도 같죠.

이 책의 후반부(Conditoned Learning)에서는 수많은 '조건'을 제시할 것입니다. 그리고 바로 옆 페이지에는 그 조건에 반응해야 하는 '뜻'을 나열해 놓겠습니다. 독자는 그저 '조건'을 보고 0.5초 이내에 뜻이 떠오르지 않을 경우, 골똘히 생각하지 말고 '뜻'을 받아쓰거나, 영단어의 뜻을 확인하여 학습하고 넘어가면 됩니다.

● 깜지의 추억

연세가 좀 있는 독자분들은 학창 시절 체벌 혹은 자습으로 깜지를 많이 해 보셨을 겁니다.

boy 소년 boy 소년 boy 소년 boy 소년 boy 소년 boy 소년 boy 소년 boy 소년
boy 소년 boy 소년 boy 소년 boy 소년 boy 소년 boy 소년 boy 소년 boy 소년
boy 소년 boy 소년 boy 소년 boy 소년 boy 소년 boy 소년…

깜지란, 이런 식으로 받아쓰는 것을 말합니다. 이런 방식의 공부는 조건화 훈련과는 전혀 다릅니다. 조건화는 조건과 반응이 동시에 주어지게 되면, 조건화되지 않는 특징을 갖기 때문입니다. 파블로프의 실험에서도 종소리와 먹이를 시간 간격 없이 동시에 강아지에게 제시했을 때에는 조건화되지 않았습니다. 즉, 종소리에 반응하지 않았죠. 또한, 깜지 학습은 집중을 하지 않으면, 학습 없이 무의식적으로 받아쓰게 됩니다.

깜지는 메타 인지 학습이 불가능합니다. 서두에 말씀드렸다시피, 메타 인지 학습은 내가 얼마나 완전하게 암기했는지, 스스로 판단하면서 하는 공부입니다. 하지만 깜지는 그 뜻이 항상 옆에 쓰여 있으므로 한 장을 가득 다 채워도 스스로 학습이 되었는지 확인할 수 없습니다.

물론 깜지도 한 장을 가득 채우면 외우게 됩니다. 모든 학습에 있어 메타 인지 학습이나 조건화보다 중요한 것은 누적 반복이기 때문입니다. 하지만 깜지는 한 장을 쓰는 내내 고도의 집중력을 요구합니다. 능동적인 집중력은 그렇게 오래가질 못합니다. 다만 깜지는 뒤에 설명할 공부법들과는 달리 멀리 우회하여 학습하지 않기 때문에, 영단어를 봤을 때 적어도 혼란이 오지는 않습니다.

● 우회 학습

영어 배움에 있어 영어권 국가에서 공부하지 않고 우리말로 해석해서 공부하는 것은 모두 우회 학습입니다. 외국어를 배울 때 학습자에게 익숙한 모국어의 개입 없이 배우려면 현지에서 그 언어와 상황을 매치시켜야 합니다. 하지만 외국에서 배우는 건 비용과 시간이 많이 들어 우리는 외국어와 우리가 쓰는 모국어를 매칭시켜 학습하는 우회 학습을 하게 되죠.

가령 'book'이라는 단어를 들었을 때, 우리는 바로 우리말로 '책'이라는 단어를 떠올립니다. 그리고 실제 책이라는 단어가 가지고 있는 의미 '종이를 여러 장 묶어 놓은 물건'을 반사적으로 떠올리죠. 'book > 책 > 종이를 여러장 묶어 놓은 물건의 이미지' 순서입니다. 그리고 실질적으로 외국어 학습을 하는 궁극적인 이유는 'book > 종이를 여러 장 묶어 놓은 물건'으로 바로 떠올리는 것입니다. 우리말의 개입을 없애 버리도록 하는 것이죠. 이 '한국어'라는 매개체를 없애야 하는데도 이미 우회하여 하는 학습을 한 번 더 우회하여 학습하는 것은 논란의 여지가 있습니다.

영단어 재우회 학습법은 대표적으로 '어원 학습법'과 '연상식 학습법'을 들 수 있는데요. 어원 학습법과 연상식 학습법은 우리 뇌의 단순 기억 기능이 아닌, 이해와 원리(어원)를 통해서 암기한다거나, 이미지나 경험(연상식 학습법)을 통해 암기를 돕습니다. 즉, 뇌의 시각 공간 또는 이해와 논리를 담당하는 부분을 활성화시키죠.

학습법 자체로만 놓고 봤을 땐 정말 훌륭한 학습법이라고 생각합니다. 장소나 이미지 혹은 이해, 논리와 합쳐진 기억은 단순 암기보다 훨씬 오래 남습니다. 하지만 이미 우회하여 하고 있는 외국어 학습에서, 그 수많은 단어를 한 번 더 우회 학습 한다는 점은 더 살펴볼 문제입니다.

● 어원 학습법

어원 학습법은 이해를 통하여 암기를 돕겠다는 취지를 가진 학습법입니다. 어원 학습법으로 학습하는 방법을 좀 더 상세히 살펴볼까요?

대표적으로 영어 접두사인 'pre'는 시간상으로 앞선다는 '미리, 일찍' 등의 뜻이 있습니다.

---

pre + face = preface = 머리말, 서문

'pre + face' 형태인 preface의 뜻은 머리말, 서문입니다. 책 앞쪽에서 먼저 머리말에 얼굴을 들이밀기 때문이라고 하는데요. 단어 하나만 봤을 땐 이해를 통하여 단어의 뜻을 유추하기에 좋은 방법이라고 할 수도 있습니다.

그렇다면, 또 다른 단어 pre 접두사가 들어가는 형태의 단어인 pretext의 뜻은 무엇일까요? 앞쪽(pre)에 글(text)이 합쳐졌으니 머리말 혹은 서문으로 해석될 수 있지 않을까요? 하지만 pretext의 뜻은 전혀 다릅니다. 변명할 말(text)를 미리(pre) 준비했다는 이유로 '핑계'나 '구실'을 뜻합니다.

또 다른 예로는 '여덟(8)'을 뜻하는 접두어 'oct'가 있습니다.

octopus	다리가 여덟 개 달린 문어
octagon	여덟 개의 꼭짓점이 있는 팔각형

자 그렇다면 October의 뜻은 무엇일까요?

아이러니하게도 October의 뜻은 10월입니다. 고대 시대의 달력에서 1년은 10개월이었습니다. 율리우스 시저가 이에 두 달을 더 추가하면서 원래 있던 명칭들이 두 달씩 밀린 건데요. 7월을 뜻하던 September(seven=sep 접두사를 가진)는 9월, 8월을 뜻하던 October는 10월, 9월을 뜻하던 November(nine=nov 접두사를가진)는 11월이 되었습니다.

언어는 영원불변하지 않습니다. 전해 내려오면서 정치, 경제, 사회, 문화 혹은 단순히 발음이 쓰기 편하다는 이유 혹은 이해하기 쉽게 하려는 이유로도 변하는 경우가 많습니다.

● 연상식(해마) 학습법

어원 학습법과 같은 재우회 학습이라고 하지만, 어원 학습법에 비해서도 훨씬 길고 꼬불꼬불한 우회로를 돌아가는 학습법인 연상식 학습법의 가치에 대해서만큼은, 다시 한번 생각해 봐야 한다고 생각합니다.

● domestic = 담(dome)을 넘어 틱(tic) 하고, 국내? 국외?

저자는 학창 시절 domestic이란 영어 단어를 연상식 학습법으로 학습한 후, 시험에서 domestic을 보고 정반대로 해석해서 틀렸던 경험이 있습니다.

domestic은 '가정의, 국내의'라는 뜻을 가진 영단어입니다.

연상식 학습법에서는 domestic이라는 영어 단어를 '담(dome)을 넘어 틱(tic) 하고 국내로 혹은 가정으로 들어오는 것'을 연상하여 외우라고 설명합니다.

저 역시 학창 시절 담을 넘는 모습을 연상하며 외웠습니다. 하지만 학습이 제대로 되지 않았는지, 담을 넘어 가정 안으로 넘어오는 것인지, 가정 밖으로 넘어가는 것인지 헷갈려 영어 해석을 전혀 다른 방향으로 하여 문제를 틀렸던 기억이 있습니다. 이처럼 연상식 학습법이 완전하지 않을 땐, 전혀 다른 방향으로 흘러갈 수 있습니다.

● 우회 학습에서 우회로를 없앨 수만 있다면

너무 극단적인 예시만으로 우회 학습을 깎아내렸다고 생각하실 수 있습니다. 우회 학습법은 앞서 설명했듯 단순 암기보다 기억이 오래간다는 장점을 이용하고, 우회하였던 길을 기억에서 인위적으로 지워 버릴 수 있다면 최고의 암기법입니다.

하지만 우리의 뇌에는 컴퓨터처럼 delete 버튼을 눌러 삭제하는 기능이 없습니다. 오히려 목적지(뜻)보다 우회로(학습법)만 집중하여 반복하다 보면, 뇌의 특성상 반사적으로 우회로만 기억날 뿐 정작 필요한 목적지(뜻)에 도착하는 시간은 훨씬 길어지거나, 엉뚱한 방향으로 나아갈 것입니다.

● 파블로프 학습법은?

언어 학습은 최대한 직관적이어야 합니다.
영단어 학습에 대한 설명이 다소 길었지만, 학습법 자체는 간단합니다.

1 영단어를 보고 뜻이 기억나지 않으면,
답을 보고 쓰도록 하여 학습을 단순화했습니다.

2 익숙한(안다는 느낌만 있지만, 뜻을 설명할 수 없는) 단어와
아는(뜻을 설명할 수 있는) 단어의 선별을 위해
끊임없이 테스트하도록 했습니다.

3 영단어의 순서조차 외우지 못하도록,
영단어가 무작위로 나오게 했습니다.

4 한 단어가 일곱 번 등장하여 누적 반복되게 하였으며,
이를 통해 장기 기억으로 전환을 돕도록 했습니다.

이 책을 학습하면서, 아래 몇 가지 사항은 꼭 유념해 주세요.

하나, 암기는 자유롭게 하지만, 지루하지는 않게.

모르는 것을 배운다! 이것은 우리의 뇌도 좋아합니다. 그러나 익숙한 것을 또 보는 것은 뇌도 지루해합니다. 그렇기에 테스트에 들어가기 전 미리 단어를 하나씩 세심하게 보는 것도 괜찮지만, 두 번 이상 보는 것은 추천하지 않습니다.

학습을 진행하다 보면 자신에게 잘 맞는 학습 방법을 발견하게 될 것입니다. 학습을 최대한 단순화시키세요!

둘, 억지로 계획을 세워 복습하지 말아 주세요.

계획적인 복습은 누적 반복하면 암기가 더 잘된다고 말하는 이론적인 내용에만 근거한 학습 지침입니다. 아직 충분히 망각되지 않은 채 같은 것을 반복했을때, 지루함을 느끼는 인간의 심리나 감정은 전혀 고려하지 않은 것이죠.

공부를 잘하려면 그냥 계획적으로 반복하면 된다고 하면서 학습에 대해 지루함이나 고됨은 그냥 정신력으로 이겨 내야 하고 그것이 안 된다면 '공부에 소질이 없는 것'이라고 치부해버립니다.

학습에서 멀어지게 하는 이 지루함들을 최대한 배제해야 합니다.
규칙적이고 계획적인 복습이 아닌, 불규칙적으로 복습하시는 것을 추천합니다. 공부했던 부분이 재미있어 다시 보고 싶거나 혹은 불현듯 호기심이 생겨 확인하고 싶은 부분이 있으면 얼마든지 복습해도 좋습니다. 하지만 그러던 중에도 지루함을 느낀다면 그냥 넘기세요.

셋, 즉각적인 복습보단 회독을 늘려라.

천천히 꼼꼼하게 빠짐없이 외우면서 책을 한 번 보고 끝내는 것보다는 여러 번 보는 것이 좋습니다. 한 번에 쉽게 외워지지 않는 부분은 다음에 다시 외운다는 생각으로 체크만 하고 넘어가세요. 또한, 되도록 책을 볼 땐, 앞으로만 공부해 나가세요(절대 대충 학습하고 넘기라는 의미는 아닙니다).
마지막 페이지까지 공부가 끝나면 다시 앞 페이지로 돌아와 다시 시작하세요.
그 어떤 과목이라도 공부를 하다 보면, 분명히 앞부분을 열심히 공부했는데 기억나지 않는 경우가 흔히 있습니다. 이때 우리는 막연한 불안감으로 다시 되짚어 보게 됩니다. 수학 교재의 집합 부분만 공부한 흔적이 명확한 것처럼 말이죠.

앞부분이 생각나지 않는 이유는 공부에 소질이 없다거나 기억력이 나빠서 그런것이 아닙니다. 이는 지극히 당연한 현상입니다. 공부했던 내용이 기억 속에서 사라져 가는 것을 자연스럽게 받아들이세요.

하루 이틀 공부해 나간 부분이 불안해서, 4~5일째 지났을 때쯤 다시 돌아가지 마세요. 책 한 권을 적어도 7~10일 정도의 주기(cycle)로 만들어, 책을 앞으로만 공부해 나가시고, 이를 한 주기로 회독을 진행하세요.
(수험용어로 책을 처음부터 끝까지 1회 끝냈을 때, 이를 '1회독'이라고 합니다.)

충분한 망각이 이루어진 후, 다시 공부하는 것이 오히려 자신의 취약 부분에 대해 확인할 기회가 됩니다. 여기서 주의할 점은 회독 주기를 너무 길게 잡지 말아야 합니다. 주기가 길어지면 제대로 학습되었던 부분마저 잊어버리게 되니, 회독 주기를 너무 길게 잡지는 말아 주세요. 7~10일 정도가 가장 좋습니다. 처음엔 7~10일 주기로 시작하지만, 학습을 더 할수록 더 빨라질 것입니다.

넷, 0.5초라고 생각하지 말고, 그냥 바로라고 생각하면 됩니다.

학습에 필요한 모든 것은 뇌가 하는 일입니다. 그날의 컨디션에 따라 0.2초에서 1초까지 다르게 반응할 수 있습니다. 너무 멀리 가지만 않으면 괜찮습니다. 그래서 0.5초라는 기준에 너무 강박 관념을 갖지 말고, 그냥 영어 단어를 보면서 바로 떠오르지 않으면 바로 뜻을 확인해 본다고 생각하면 됩니다. 눈을 빨리 돌릴 필요도 없고, 고개를 빨리 돌릴 필요도 없습니다. 공부하는 데 있어서, 스스로 스트레스를 주지 마세요. 그냥 영단어를 보고 뜻이 생각나지 않는다면, 그냥 자연스럽게 눈을 돌려서 뜻을 확인하는 것입니다.

다섯, 뜻을 확인한 후엔 받아쓰는 것을 추천합니다.

글자를 그대로 옮겨 쓰는 필사는 최고의 공부 방법 중 하나입니다.

필사를 하는 동안 스펠링 확인을 위해 영단어를 적어도 세 번 이상, 뜻도 세 번 이상 무의식적으로 보게 되기 때문이죠.

여섯, 체크하면서 공부해 주세요.

만약 뜻을 쓸 수 없다면, 되도록 ○, ×라도 꼭 표시해 주세요.

공부하는 데 가장 어려운 것은 시작하는 것입니다. 이전에 학습을 어디까지 했는지 기억나지 않는 것도 학습에 있어 스트레스입니다.

일곱, 너무 철저한 계획보다는 지킬 수 있는 유연한 계획을 세우세요.

물론 매일 열 페이지씩 혹은 스무 페이지씩 공부하겠다는 계획을 세워 실천하는 것도 좋습니다. 하지만 다양한 변수들로 인해 그 계획이 한번 무너지면, 그 뒤에 세워 두었던 계획들까지 우르르 무너지는 경우가 많습니다.

차라리 평소 공부 계획을 세우지 않은 상태에서, 컨디션이 좋은 날 많이 공부하고, 컨디션이 좋지 않은 날은 적게 공부하며 스트레스를 받지 않는 편이 낫습니다.

다만, 하루 한 페이지라도 좋으니, 매일 공부하는 습관만 들이세요. 한 페이지만 보려고 시작해 버리면, 오히려 열 페이지 또는 스무 페이지까지 공부하게 되는 경우가 많습니다. '최소한 한 페이지라도 보겠다!'라는 현실적인 계획이 좋습니다.

그 외

본 교재의 학습(Conditioned Learning) 부분은 스프링 제본해서 공부하시는 것을 추천합니다. 공부하면서 책의 페이지가 자꾸 넘어오는 것 또한 공부에 집중하지 못하게 만들며, 스트레스를 받는 요인 중 하나입니다.

공부를 대충대충 하라는 의미가 아닙니다.

최소한 영단어를 보고 이게 무슨 단어일지 생각은 해 보셔야 합니다. 0.5초 안에 생각나지 않는다면 학습되지 않은 것으로 간주하는 것이지, 보자마자 영단어의 뜻이 무엇일까 하는 스스로 물음도 없이 무의식적으로 뜻을 보고 받아쓰면 안됩니다.

뜻이 기억나지 않더라도 '이게 무슨 뜻일까?'라는 의문은 가져야 합니다. 다만 스트레스를 받지 않는 선에서 말이죠. 기억나지 않을 땐, 그때마다 ㅇ, × 등의 표기를 해두고, 뜻을 필기하고 넘기라는 뜻입니다.

본 교재의 학습법으로 여러분들이 영어 단어뿐만 아니라, 모든 학습에 있어 흥미를 느낄 수 있기를 바랍니다.

02.

Conditioned
Learning

외우는 게 지루하면 바로 다음 페이지로 넘어가세요!

abandon [əbaéndən]	버리다
compensate [kʌ́mpənsèit]	보상하다
extinguish [ikstíŋgwiʃ]	끄다
beloved [bilʌ́vid]	총애받는
agriculture [aégrəkʌ̀ltʃər]	농업
dense [dens]	빽빽한
custom [kʌ́stəm]	관습
voyage [vɔ́iidʒ]	항해
reap [riːp]	거두다, 수확하다
annoy [ənɔ́i]	짜증 나게 하다

뜻이 바로 떠오르지 않으면 왼쪽 페이지의 뜻을 보고 적으세요.

abandon		compensate	
agriculture		extinguish	
dense		annoy	
compensate		custom	
voyage		reap	
annoy		abandon	
beloved		annoy	
extinguish		custom	
reap		reap	
abandon		agriculture	
dense		dense	
custom		beloved	
extinguish		compensate	
reap		extinguish	
abandon		voyage	
dense		abandon	
custom		annoy	
extinguish		custom	
beloved		reap	
agriculture		agriculture	
compensate		dense	
reap		beloved	
voyage		compensate	
annoy		extinguish	
abandon		voyage	
voyage		abandon	
agriculture		agriculture	
custom		dense	
reap		compensate	
annoy		custom	
extinguish		voyage	
dense		annoy	
compensate		beloved	
beloved		extinguish	
abandon		reap	

외우는 게 지루하면 바로 다음 페이지로 넘어가세요!

broad [brɔːd]	넓은
district [dístrikt]	구역
interest [íntərəst]	흥미, 호기심
overwhelm [òuvərhwélm]	휩싸다, 제압하다
intellectual [ìntəléktʃuəl]	지능의, 지적인
praise [preiz]	칭찬하다
omit [oumít]	빠뜨리다, 누락시키다
recover [rikʌ́vər]	회복하다
shame [ʃeim]	수치심
identity [aidéntəti]	신분, 정체성

뜻이 바로 떠오르지 않으면 왼쪽 페이지의 뜻을 보고 적으세요.

broad	_____	district	_____
intellectual	_____	interest	_____
praise	_____	identity	_____
district	_____	omit	_____
omit	_____	shame	_____
recover	_____	broad	_____
identity	_____	identity	_____
overwhelm	_____	omit	_____
interest	_____	shame	_____
shame	_____	intellectual	_____
broad	_____	praise	_____
praise	_____	overwhelm	_____
omit	_____	district	_____
interest	_____	interest	_____
overwhelm	_____	recover	_____
intellectual	_____	broad	_____
district	_____	identity	_____
shame	_____	omit	_____
recover	_____	shame	_____
identity	_____	intellectual	_____
broad	_____	praise	_____
recover	_____	overwhelm	_____
intellectual	_____	district	_____
omit	_____	interest	_____
shame	_____	recover	_____
identity	_____	broad	_____
interest	_____	intellectual	_____
praise	_____	praise	_____
district	_____	district	_____
overwhelm	_____	omit	_____
broad	_____	recover	_____
recover	_____	identity	_____
praise	_____	overwhelm	_____
overwhelm	_____	interest	_____
intellectual	_____	shame	_____

외우는 게 지루하면 바로 다음 페이지로 넘어가세요!

summary [sʌ́məri]	요약
mankind [mǽnkaínd]	인류
plot [plat]	줄거리, 구성
damp [dæmp]	축축한
resist [rizíst]	저항하다
introduce [ìntrədjúːs]	소개하다
confer [kənfə́ːr]	상의하다
trivial [tríviəl]	사소한, 하찮은
vessel [vésəl]	선박
dialect [dáiəlèkt]	방언, 사투리

뜻이 바로 떠오르지 않으면 왼쪽 페이지의 뜻을 보고 적으세요.

summary		mankind	
resist		plot	
introduce		dialect	
mankind		confer	
confer		vessel	
trivial		summary	
dialect		dialect	
damp		confer	
plot		vessel	
vessel		resist	
summary		introduce	
introduce		damp	
confer		mankind	
plot		plot	
damp		trivial	
resist		summary	
mankind		dialect	
vessel		confer	
trivial		vessel	
dialect		resist	
summary		introduce	
trivial		damp	
resist		mankind	
confer		plot	
vessel		trivial	
dialect		summary	
plot		resist	
introduce		introduce	
mankind		mankind	
damp		confer	
summary		trivial	
trivial		dialect	
introduce		damp	
damp		plot	
resist		vessel	

외우는 게 지루하면 바로 다음 페이지로 넘어가세요!

worth [wəːrθ]	가치가 있는
cooperate [kouápərèit]	협력하다
legal [líːgəl]	합법적인
drastic [draéstik]	과감한
prescribe [priskráib]	처방하다
sour [sauər]	시큼한
allow [əláu]	허락하다
notify [nóutəfài]	알리다
capture [kaéptʃər]	억류하다, 포획하다
surround [səráund]	둘러싸다

뜻이 바로 떠오르지 않으면 왼쪽 페이지의 뜻을 보고 적으세요.

worth		cooperate	
prescribe		legal	
sour		surround	
cooperate		allow	
allow		capture	
notify		worth	
surround		surround	
drastic		allow	
legal		capture	
capture		prescribe	
worth		sour	
sour		drastic	
allow		cooperate	
legal		legal	
drastic		notify	
prescribe		worth	
cooperate		surround	
capture		allow	
notify		capture	
surround		prescribe	
worth		sour	
notify		drastic	
prescribe		cooperate	
allow		legal	
capture		notify	
surround		worth	
legal		prescribe	
sour		sour	
cooperate		cooperate	
drastic		allow	
worth		notify	
notify		surround	
sour		drastic	
drastic		legal	
prescribe		capture	

arise [əráiz]	생기다, 발생하다
twilight [twáilàit]	황혼
preach [pri:tʃ]	설교하다
convention [kənvénʃən]	관습
somewhat [sʌ́mhwʌt]	어느 정도, 약간
specimen [spésəmən]	견본, 샘플
lecture [léktʃər]	강의
currency [kə́:rənsi]	통화, 통용
demand [dimaénd]	요구, 요청
pastime [paéstàim]	취미

뜻이 바로 떠오르지 않으면 왼쪽 페이지의 뜻을 보고 적으세요.

arise		twilight	
somewhat		preach	
specimen		pastime	
twilight		lecture	
lecture		demand	
currency		arise	
pastime		pastime	
convention		lecture	
preach		demand	
demand		somewhat	
arise		specimen	
specimen		convention	
lecture		twilight	
preach		preach	
convention		currency	
somewhat		arise	
twilight		pastime	
demand		lecture	
currency		demand	
pastime		somewhat	
arise		specimen	
currency		convention	
somewhat		twilight	
lecture		preach	
demand		currency	
pastime		arise	
preach		somewhat	
specimen		specimen	
twilight		Iwilight	
convention		lecture	
arise		currency	
currency		pastime	
specimen		convention	
convention		preach	
somewhat		demand	

외우는 게 지루하면 바로 다음 페이지로 넘어가세요!

fate [feit]	운명
refuse [rifjú:z]	거절하다
discern [disə́:rn]	알아차리다
commute [kəmjú:t]	감형하다, 대체하다
trail [treil]	자국, 자취
evolve [iválv]	진화하다, 발달하다
ruin [rú:in]	망치다
throne [θroun]	왕좌
medium [mí:diəm]	매체, 중간의
assign [əsáin]	선임하다, 맡기다

뜻이 바로 떠오르지 않으면 왼쪽 페이지의 뜻을 보고 적으세요.

fate		refuse	
trail		discern	
evolve		assign	
refuse		ruin	
ruin		medium	
throne		fate	
assign		assign	
commute		ruin	
discern		medium	
medium		trail	
fate		evolve	
evolve		commute	
ruin		refuse	
discern		discern	
commute		throne	
trail		fate	
refuse		assign	
medium		ruin	
throne		medium	
assign		trail	
fate		evolve	
throne		commute	
trail		refuse	
ruin		discern	
medium		throne	
assign		fate	
discern		trail	
evolve		evolve	
refuse		refuse	
commute		ruin	
fate		throne	
throne		assign	
evolve		commute	
commute		discern	
trail		medium	

foster [fɔ́:stər]	조성하다
supplement [sʌ́pləmənt]	보충
celebrate [séləbrèit]	기념하다, 축하하다
content [kántent]	내용물
induce [-indjúːst]	유도하다
rough [rʌf]	거친
revenge [rivéndʒ]	복수
fundamental [fʌndəméntl]	근본적인
seed [siːd]	씨, 씨앗
estate [istéit]	사유지

뜻이 바로 떠오르지 않으면 왼쪽 페이지의 뜻을 보고 적으세요.

foster		supplement	
induce		celebrate	
rough		estate	
supplement		revenge	
revenge		seed	
fundamental		foster	
estate		estate	
content		revenge	
celebrate		seed	
seed		induce	
foster		rough	
rough		content	
revenge		supplement	
celebrate		celebrate	
content		fundamental	
induce		foster	
supplement		estate	
seed		revenge	
fundamental		seed	
estate		induce	
foster		rough	
fundamental		content	
induce		supplement	
revenge		celebrate	
seed		fundamental	
estate		foster	
celebrate		induce	
rough		rough	
supplement		supplement	
content		revenge	
foster		fundamental	
fundamental		estate	
rough		content	
content		celebrate	
induce		seed	

외우는 게 지루하면 바로 다음 페이지로 넘어가세요!

limit [límit]	한도, 제한
nevertheless [nèvərðəlés]	그럼에도 불구하고
enterprise [éntərpràiz]	기업, 회사
proficient [prəfíʃənt]	능숙한
assume [əsúːm]	추정하다
gradual [graédʒuəl]	점진적인
career [kaériər]	직업
grateful [gréitfəl]	감사하는
human [hjúːmən]	인간의
define [difáin]	정의하다

뜻이 바로 떠오르지 않으면 왼쪽 페이지의 뜻을 보고 적으세요.

limit	nevertheless
assume	enterprise
gradual	define
nevertheless	career
career	human
grateful	limit
define	define
proficient	career
enterprise	human
human	assume
limit	gradual
gradual	proficient
career	nevertheless
enterprise	enterprise
proficient	grateful
assume	limit
nevertheless	define
human	career
grateful	human
define	assume
limit	gradual
grateful	proficient
assume	nevertheless
career	enterprise
human	grateful
define	limit
enterprise	assume
gradual	gradual
nevertheless	nevertheless
proficient	career
limit	grateful
grateful	define
gradual	proficient
proficient	enterprise
assume	human

외우는 게 지루하면 바로 다음 페이지로 넘어가세요!

complicate [kámpləkèit]	악화시키다
narrate [naéreit]	이야기하다
reduce [ridjú:s]	줄이다, 낮추다
cultivate [kʌltəvèit]	경작하다, 일구다
external [ikstə́:rnl]	외부의, 밖의
congress [káŋgris]	의회, 회의
dominate [dámənèit]	지배하다
cordial [kɔ́:rdʒəl]	화기애애한, 다정한
acquaint [əkwéint]	익히다, 숙지하다
advance [ædvaéns]	발전, 진전

뜻이 바로 떠오르지 않으면 왼쪽 페이지의 뜻을 보고 적으세요.

complicate		narrate
external		reduce
congress		advance
narrate		dominate
dominate		acquaint
cordial		complicate
advance		advance
cultivate		dominate
reduce		acquaint
acquaint		external
complicate		congress
congress		cultivate
dominate		narrate
reduce		reduce
cultivate		cordial
external		complicate
narrate		advance
acquaint		dominate
cordial		acquaint
advance		external
complicate		congress
cordial		cultivate
external		narrate
dominate		reduce
acquaint		cordial
advance		complicate
reduce		external
congress		congress
narrate		narrate
cultivate		dominate
complicate		cordial
cordial		advance
congress		cultivate
cultivate		reduce
external		acquaint

외우는 게 지루하면 바로 다음 페이지로 넘어가세요!

horn [hɔːrn]	뿔
eventually [ivéntʃuəli]	결국, 끝내
rebel [rɪbél]	반역자
sting [stiŋ]	찌르다
ignore [ignɔ́ːr]	무시하다
confront [kənfrʌnt]	닥치다, 직면하다
authority [əθɔ́ːrətii]	권한
miracle [mírəkl]	기적
poverty [pávərti]	가난
discharge [distʃáːrdʒ]	해고하다, 석방하다

뜻이 바로 떠오르지 않으면 왼쪽 페이지의 뜻을 보고 적으세요.

horn		eventually	
ignore		rebel	
confront		discharge	
eventually		authority	
authority		poverty	
miracle		horn	
discharge		discharge	
sting		authority	
rebel		poverty	
poverty		ignore	
horn		confront	
confront		sting	
authority		eventually	
rebel		rebel	
sting		miracle	
ignore		horn	
eventually		discharge	
poverty		authority	
miracle		poverty	
discharge		ignore	
horn		confront	
miracle		sting	
ignore		eventually	
authority		rebel	
poverty		miracle	
discharge		horn	
rebel		ignore	
confront		confront	
eventually		eventually	
sting		authority	
horn		miracle	
miracle		discharge	
confront		sting	
sting		rebel	
ignore		poverty	

외우는 게 지루하면 바로 다음 페이지로 넘어가세요!

tragic [traédʒik]	비극적인, 비극의
incident [ínsədənt]	사고, 사건
renew [rinjú:]	재개하다, 갱신하다
accumulate [əkjú:mjulèit]	축적하다, 모으다
eminent [émənənt]	저명한
degrade [digréid]	비하하다
deliberate [dilíbərət]	의도적인
medieval [mì:díí:vəl]	중세의
cliff [klif]	절벽
worship [wə́:rʃip]	숭배

뜻이 바로 떠오르지 않으면 왼쪽 페이지의 뜻을 보고 적으세요.

tragic		incident	
eminent		renew	
degrade		worship	
incident		deliberate	
deliberate		cliff	
medieval		tragic	
worship		worship	
accumulate		deliberate	
renew		cliff	
cliff		eminent	
tragic		degrade	
degrade		accumulate	
deliberate		incident	
renew		renew	
accumulate		medieval	
eminent		tragic	
incident		worship	
cliff		deliberate	
medieval		cliff	
worship		eminent	
tragic		degrade	
medieval		accumulate	
eminent		incident	
deliberate		renew	
cliff		medieval	
worship		tragic	
renew		eminent	
degrade		degrade	
incident		incidcnt	
accumulate		deliberate	
tragic		medieval	
medieval		worship	
degrade		accumulate	
accumulate		renew	
eminent		cliff	

외우는 게 지루하면 바로 다음 페이지로 넘어가세요!

weave [wiːv]	(맛이) 짜다
unite [juːnáit]	연합하다
dismiss [dismís]	묵살하다, 해고하다
locate [lóukeit]	위치하다
rid [rid]	없애다
dignity [dígnəti]	위엄
theory [θíːəri]	이론
gloomy [glúːmi]	우울한
stuff [stʌf]	물건
section [sékʃən]	부분, 구획

뜻이 바로 떠오르지 않으면 왼쪽 페이지의 뜻을 보고 적으세요.

weave		unite	
rid		dismiss	
dignity		section	
unite		theory	
theory		stuff	
gloomy		weave	
section		section	
locate		theory	
dismiss		stuff	
stuff		rid	
weave		dignity	
dignity		locate	
theory		unite	
dismiss		dismiss	
locate		gloomy	
rid		weave	
unite		section	
stuff		theory	
gloomy		stuff	
section		rid	
weave		dignity	
gloomy		locate	
rid		unite	
theory		dismiss	
stuff		gloomy	
section		weave	
dismiss		rid	
dignity		dignity	
unite		unitc	
locate		theory	
weave		gloomy	
gloomy		section	
dignity		locate	
locate		dismiss	
rid		stuff	

외우는 게 지루하면 바로 다음 페이지로 넘어가세요!

inspect [inspékt]	점검하다
adventure [ædvéntʃər]	모험
decorate [dékərèit]	장식하다, 꾸미다
principal [prínsəpəl]	주요한
diminish [dimíniʃ]	줄어들다
sole [soul]	혼자의, 유일한
flourish [fláːriʃ]	번창하다
neglect [niglékt]	방치하다
fascinate [fǽsənèit]	매혹하다
vacuum [vǽkjuəm]	진공

inspect		adventure	
diminish		decorate	
sole		vacuum	
adventure		flourish	
flourish		fascinate	
neglect		inspect	
vacuum		vacuum	
principal		flourish	
decorate		fascinate	
fascinate		diminish	
inspect		sole	
sole		principal	
flourish		adventure	
decorate		decorate	
principal		neglect	
diminish		inspect	
adventure		vacuum	
fascinate		flourish	
neglect		fascinate	
vacuum		diminish	
inspect		sole	
neglect		principal	
diminish		adventure	
flourish		decorate	
fascinate		neglect	
vacuum		inspect	
decorate		diminish	
sole		sole	
adventure		adventure	
principal		flourish	
inspect		neglect	
neglect		vacuum	
sole		principal	
principal		decorate	
diminish		fascinate	

외우는 게 지루하면 바로 다음 페이지로 넘어가세요!

sensitive [sénsətiv]	예민한
rob [rab]	빼앗다, 털다
outstanding [auˌtstæˈndiŋ]	뛰어난
chaos [kéias]	혼돈
contest [kántest]	대회
satellite [saétəlàit]	위성
beard [biərd]	턱수염
visible [vízəbl]	보이는
tension [ténʃən]	긴장
prepare [pripéər]	준비하다

뜻이 바로 떠오르지 않으면 왼쪽 페이지의 뜻을 보고 적으세요.

sensitive		rob	
contest		outstanding	
satellite		prepare	
rob		beard	
beard		tension	
visible		sensitive	
prepare		prepare	
chaos		beard	
outstanding		tension	
tension		contest	
sensitive		satellite	
satellite		chaos	
beard		rob	
outstanding		outstanding	
chaos		visible	
contest		sensitive	
rob		prepare	
tension		beard	
visible		tension	
prepare		contest	
sensitive		satellite	
visible		chaos	
contest		rob	
beard		outstanding	
tension		visible	
prepare		sensitive	
outstanding		contest	
satellite		satellite	
rob		rob	
chaos		beard	
sensitive		visible	
visible		prepare	
satellite		chaos	
chaos		outstanding	
contest		tension	

외우는 게 지루하면 바로 다음 페이지로 넘어가세요!

priceless [práislis]	귀중한
delay [diléi]	연기하다
modify [mádəfài]	수정하다
import [impɔ́ːrt]	수입품
monotonous [mənátənəs]	단조로운
nourish [nə́ːriʃ]	키우다
imperial [impíəriəl]	제국의, 황제의
partial [páːrʃəl]	부분적인, 편파적인
instant [ínstənt]	즉시, 즉각적인
approach [əpróutʃ]	접근

뜻이 바로 떠오르지 않으면 왼쪽 페이지의 뜻을 보고 적으세요.

priceless		delay	
monotonous		modify	
nourish		approach	
delay		imperial	
imperial		instant	
partial		priceless	
approach		approach	
import		imperial	
modify		instant	
instant		monotonous	
priceless		nourish	
nourish		import	
imperial		delay	
modify		modify	
import		partial	
monotonous		priceless	
delay		approach	
instant		imperial	
partial		instant	
approach		monotonous	
priceless		nourish	
partial		import	
monotonous		delay	
imperial		modify	
instant		partial	
approach		priceless	
modify		monotonous	
nourish		nourish	
delay		delay	
import		imperial	
priceless		partial	
partial		approach	
nourish		import	
import		modify	
monotonous		instant	

외우는 게 지루하면 바로 다음 페이지로 넘어가세요!

ideal [aidíːəl]	이상적인
selfish [sélfiʃ]	이기적인
ecology [ikálədʒi]	생태학
associate [əsóuʃièit]	연관 짓다
form [fɔːrm]	종류, 형태
transfer [trænsfə́ːr]	갈아타다
concern [kənsə́ːrn]	걱정하다
interval [íntərvəl]	간격
patient [péiʃənt]	환자
appeal [əpíːl]	간청하다, 항소하다

뜻이 바로 떠오르지 않으면 왼쪽 페이지의 뜻을 보고 적으세요.

ideal		selfish	
form		ecology	
transfer		appeal	
selfish		concern	
concern		patient	
interval		ideal	
appeal		appeal	
associate		concern	
ecology		patient	
patient		form	
ideal		transfer	
transfer		associate	
concern		selfish	
ecology		ecology	
associate		interval	
form		ideal	
selfish		appeal	
patient		concern	
interval		patient	
appeal		form	
ideal		transfer	
interval		associate	
form		selfish	
concern		ecology	
patient		interval	
appeal		ideal	
ecology		form	
transfer		transfer	
selfish		selfish	
associate		concern	
ideal		interval	
interval		appeal	
transfer		associate	
associate		ecology	
form		patient	

외우는 게 지루하면 바로 다음 페이지로 넘어가세요!

moisture [mɔ́istʃər]	수분, 습기
mature [mətjúər]	성숙한
substance [sʌ́bstəns]	물질
withstand [wiðstaénd]	견디다
vanish [vaéniʃ]	사라지다
constitution [kánstətjúːʃən]	헌법
aim [eim]	목적, 목표
frown [fraun]	찌푸리다
shelter [ʃéltər]	주거지, 대피처
advertise [aédvərtàiz]	광고하다

뜻이 바로 떠오르지 않으면 왼쪽 페이지의 뜻을 보고 적으세요.

moisture		mature	
vanish		substance	
constitution		advertise	
mature		aim	
aim		shelter	
frown		moisture	
advertise		advertise	
withstand		aim	
substance		shelter	
shelter		vanish	
moisture		constitution	
constitution		withstand	
aim		mature	
substance		substance	
withstand		frown	
vanish		moisture	
mature		advertise	
shelter		aim	
frown		shelter	
advertise		vanish	
moisture		constitution	
frown		withstand	
vanish		mature	
aim		substance	
shelter		frown	
advertise		moisture	
substance		vanish	
constitution		constitution	
mature		mature	
withstand		aim	
moisture		frown	
frown		advertise	
constitution		withstand	
withstand		substance	
vanish		shelter	

외우는 게 지루하면 바로 다음 페이지로 넘어가세요!

derive [diráiv]	끌어내다, 얻다
appropriate [əpróupriət]	적절한
scheme [ski:m]	계획
seize [si:z]	붙잡다
counsel [káunsəl]	상담
efficient [ifíʃənt]	효과적인, 효능 있는
embarrass [imbaérəs]	당황하다, 부끄럽게 하다
conference [kánfərəns]	회견, 회의
aspect [aéspekt]	양상, 측면
artificial [á:rtəfíʃəl]	인공의, 인위적인

derive		appropriate	
counsel		scheme	
efficient		artificial	
appropriate		embarrass	
embarrass		aspect	
conference		derive	
artificial		artificial	
seize		embarrass	
scheme		aspect	
aspect		counsel	
derive		efficient	
efficient		seize	
embarrass		appropriate	
scheme		scheme	
seize		conference	
counsel		derive	
appropriate		artificial	
aspect		embarrass	
conference		aspect	
artificial		counsel	
derive		efficient	
conference		seize	
counsel		appropriate	
embarrass		scheme	
aspect		conference	
artificial		derive	
scheme		counsel	
efficient		efficient	
appropriate		appropriate	
seize		embarrass	
derive		conference	
conference		artificial	
efficient		seize	
seize		scheme	
counsel		aspect	

외우는 게 지루하면 바로 다음 페이지로 넘어가세요!

involve [inválv]	포함하다, 말려들게 되다
criticize [krítəsàiz]	비난하다, 비판하다
peel [piːl]	벗기다
perform [pərfɔ́ːrm]	수행하다, 공연하다
suicide [sjúːəsàid]	자살하다, 자멸하다
include [inklúːd]	포함하다, 함유하다
collect [inklúːd]	모으다, 수집하다
offend [əfénd]	불쾌하게 하다
astronomy [əstránəmi]	천문학
profound [prəfáund]	심오한, 깊은

뜻이 바로 떠오르지 않으면 왼쪽 페이지의 뜻을 보고 적으세요.

involve		appropriate	
suicide		scheme	
include		artificial	
criticize		embarrass	
collect		aspect	
offend		derive	
profound		artificial	
perform		embarrass	
peel		aspect	
astronomy		counsel	
involve		efficient	
include		seize	
collect		appropriate	
peel		scheme	
perform		conference	
suicide		derive	
criticize		artificial	
astronomy		embarrass	
offend		aspect	
profound		counsel	
involve		efficient	
offend		seize	
suicide		appropriate	
collect		scheme	
astronomy		conference	
profound		derive	
peel		counsel	
include		criticize	
criticize		peel	
perform		profound	
involve		collect	
offend		astronomy	
include		involve	
perform		profound	
suicide		collect	

63

외우는 게 지루하면 바로 다음 페이지로 넘어가세요!

superior [səpíəriər]	우수한, 위의
category [kaétəgɔ̀:ri]	범주, 분류
invest [invést]	투자하다, 투입하다
anniversary [ænəvə́:rsəri]	기념일
diverse [divə́:rs]	다양한, 다른
raw [rɔ:]	익히지 않은, 날것의
similar [símələr]	비슷한, 유사한
creep [kri:p]	기어가다
forbid [fərbíd]	금지하다
collapse [kəlaéps]	붕괴하다, 무너지다

뜻이 바로 떠오르지 않으면 왼쪽 페이지의 뜻을 보고 적으세요.

superior		category	
diverse		invest	
raw		collapse	
category		similar	
similar		forbid	
creep		superior	
collapse		collapse	
anniversary		similar	
invest		forbid	
forbid		diverse	
superior		raw	
raw		anniversary	
similar		category	
invest		invest	
anniversary		creep	
diverse		superior	
category		collapse	
forbid		similar	
creep		forbid	
collapse		diverse	
superior		raw	
creep		anniversary	
diverse		category	
similar		invest	
forbid		creep	
collapse		superior	
invest		diverse	
raw		raw	
category		category	
anniversary		similar	
superior		creep	
creep		collapse	
raw		anniversary	
anniversary		invest	
diverse		forbid	

외우는 게 지루하면 바로 다음 페이지로 넘어가세요!

mock [mak]	조롱하다
resign [rizáin]	사임, 사퇴
previous [príːviəs]	이전의, 앞선
torment [tɔːrmént]	고통, 괴롭히다
crew [kruː]	승무원, 선원
bloom [bluːm]	꽃이 피다, 개화
injure [índʒər]	상처를 입히다
scatter [skaétər]	흩어지다
extraordinary [ikstrɔ́ː]	특별한, 뛰어난
resent [rizént]	분개하다, 싫어하다

뜻이 바로 떠오르지 않으면 왼쪽 페이지의 뜻을 보고 적으세요.

mock		resign	
crew		previous	
bloom		resent	
resign		injure	
injure		extraordinary	
scatter		mock	
resent		resent	
torment		injure	
previous		extraordinary	
extraordinary		crew	
mock		bloom	
bloom		torment	
injure		resign	
previous		previous	
torment		scatter	
crew		mock	
resign		resent	
extraordinary		injure	
scatter		extraordinary	
resent		crew	
mock		bloom	
scatter		torment	
crew		resign	
injure		previous	
extraordinary		scatter	
resent		mock	
previous		crew	
bloom		bloom	
resign		resign	
torment		injure	
mock		scatter	
scatter		resent	
bloom		torment	
torment		previous	
crew		extraordinary	

외우는 게 지루하면 바로 다음 페이지로 넘어가세요!

clay [klei]	점토, 진흙
incline [inkláin]	기울다, ~할 마음이 생기다
grab [græb]	붙들다, 움켜쥐다
depict [dipíkt]	묘사하다, 그리다
tongue [tʌŋ]	혀, 말
starve [staːrv]	굶기다, 굶주리다
globe [gloub]	세계, 지구
explanation [èksplənéiʃən]	설명, 해명
solitary [sálətèri]	혼자의, 외딴
accurate [aékjurət]	정확한, 정밀한

뜻이 바로 떠오르지 않으면 왼쪽 페이지의 뜻을 보고 적으세요.

clay		incline	
tongue		grab	
starve		accurate	
incline		globe	
globe		solitary	
explanation		clay	
accurate		accurate	
depict		globe	
grab		solitary	
solitary		tongue	
clay		starve	
starve		depict	
globe		incline	
grab		grab	
depict		explanation	
tongue		clay	
incline		accurate	
solitary		globe	
explanation		solitary	
accurate		tongue	
clay		starve	
explanation		depict	
tongue		incline	
globe		grab	
solitary		explanation	
accurate		clay	
grab		tongue	
starve		starve	
incline		incline	
depict		globe	
clay		explanation	
explanation		accurate	
starve		depict	
depict		grab	
tongue		solitary	

외우는 게 지루하면 바로 다음 페이지로 넘어가세요!

annual [aénjuəl]	연간의, 연례의
avoid [əvɔ́id]	피하다, 회피하다
convince [kənvíns]	설득하다, 확신시키다
civilization [sìvəli-zéiʃən]	문명
doom [du:m]	운명, 파멸
closet [klázit]	벽장
admire [ædmáiər]	존경하다, 감탄하다
divide [diváid]	나누다, 분할하다
frank [fræŋk]	솔직한
accommodate [əkámədèit]	수용하다, 편의를 도모하다

뜻이 바로 떠오르지 않으면 왼쪽 페이지의 뜻을 보고 적으세요.

annual		avoid	
doom		convince	
closet		accommodate	
avoid		admire	
admire		frank	
divide		annual	
accommodate		accommodate	
civilization		admire	
convince		frank	
frank		doom	
annual		closet	
closet		civilization	
admire		avoid	
convince		convince	
civilization		divide	
doom		annual	
avoid		accommodate	
frank		admire	
divide		frank	
accommodate		doom	
annual		closet	
divide		civilization	
doom		avoid	
admire		convince	
frank		divide	
accommodate		annual	
convince		doom	
closet		closet	
avoid		avoid	
civilization		admire	
annual		divide	
divide		accommodate	
closet		civilization	
civilization		convince	
doom		frank	

외우는 게 지루하면 바로 다음 페이지로 넘어가세요!

discipline [dísəplin]	훈련, 훈련하다
amount [əmáunt]	총액, 총계
temporary [témpərèri]	일시적인, 임시의
paragraph [pǽrəgrǽf]	단락, 문단
apparatus [æpərǽtəs]	장치, 기구
income [ínkʌm]	소득, 수입
grain [grein]	곡물
charity [tʃǽrəti]	자선
consequence [kánsəkwèns]	결과
majority [mədʒɔ́ːrəti]	다수, 대부분

뜻이 바로 떠오르지 않으면 왼쪽 페이지의 뜻을 보고 적으세요.

discipline		amount	
apparatus		temporary	
income		majority	
amount		grain	
grain		consequence	
charity		discipline	
majority		majority	
paragraph		grain	
temporary		consequence	
consequence		apparatus	
discipline		income	
income		paragraph	
grain		amount	
temporary		temporary	
paragraph		charity	
apparatus		discipline	
amount		majority	
consequence		grain	
charity		consequence	
majority		apparatus	
discipline		income	
charity		paragraph	
apparatus		amount	
grain		temporary	
consequence		charity	
majority		discipline	
temporary		apparatus	
income		income	
amount		amount	
paragraph		grain	
discipline		charity	
charity		majority	
income		paragraph	
paragraph		temporary	
apparatus		consequence	

외우는 게 지루하면 바로 다음 페이지로 넘어가세요!

colleague [káli:g]	동료
disgust [disgʌst]	혐오, 메스꺼움
supervise [sú:pərvàiz]	감독하다, 관리하다
steady [stédi]	지속적인, 안정된
argue [á:rgju:]	주장하다
private [práivət]	개인의, 사적인
guarantee [gærəntí:]	보장하다, 보증
continent [kántənənt]	대륙
bride [braid]	신부
status [stéitəs]	상태, 지위

뜻이 바로 떠오르지 않으면 왼쪽 페이지의 뜻을 보고 적으세요.

colleague		disgust	
argue		supervise	
private		status	
disgust		guarantee	
guarantee		bride	
continent		colleague	
status		status	
steady		guarantee	
supervise		bride	
bride		argue	
colleague		private	
private		steady	
guarantee		disgust	
supervise		supervise	
steady		continent	
argue		colleague	
disgust		status	
bride		guarantee	
continent		bride	
status		argue	
colleague		private	
continent		steady	
argue		disgust	
guarantee		supervise	
bride		continent	
status		colleague	
supervise		argue	
private		private	
disgust		disgust	
steady		guarantee	
colleague		continent	
continent		status	
private		steady	
steady		supervise	
argue		bride	

외우는 게 지루하면 바로 다음 페이지로 넘어가세요!

vital [váitl]	필수적인, 활력이 넘치는
enrich [inrítʃ]	부유하게 하다
priest [pri:st]	신부, 사제
channel [tʃaénl]	경로, 통로
refine [rifáin]	정제하다, 개선하다
adopt [ədápt]	입양하다, 채택하다
addict [aédikt]	중독되다
role [roul]	역할, 임무
sweep [swi:p]	휩쓸다, 압승하다
usage [jú:sidʒ]	사용, 용법

뜻이 바로 떠오르지 않으면 왼쪽 페이지의 뜻을 보고 적으세요.

vital			enrich		
refine			priest		
adopt			usage		
enrich			addict		
addict			sweep		
role			vital		
usage			usage		
channel			addict		
priest			sweep		
sweep			refine		
vital			adopt		
adopt			channel		
addict			enrich		
priest			priest		
channel			role		
refine			vital		
enrich			usage		
sweep			addict		
role			sweep		
usage			refine		
vital			adopt		
role			channel		
refine			enrich		
addict			priest		
sweep			role		
usage			vital		
priest			refine		
adopt			adopt		
enrich			enrich		
channel			addict		
vital			role		
role			usage		
adopt			channel		
channel			priest		
refine			sweep		

exclaim [ikskléim]	외치다, 감탄하다
popular [pápjulər]	인기 있는
direct [dirékt]	직접적인
roar [rɔːr]	소리 지르다
belong [bilɔ́ːŋ]	속하다, ~의 것이다
molecule [máləkjùːl]	분자
tiny [táini]	작은, 조금
tidy [táidi]	정리하다, 깨끗한
planet [plaénit]	행성, 유성
article [áːrtikl]	논문, 기사

뜻이 바로 떠오르지 않으면 왼쪽 페이지의 뜻을 보고 적으세요.

exclaim		popular	
belong		direct	
molecule		article	
popular		tiny	
tiny		planet	
tidy		exclaim	
article		article	
roar		tiny	
direct		planet	
planet		belong	
exclaim		molecule	
molecule		roar	
tiny		popular	
direct		direct	
roar		tidy	
belong		exclaim	
popular		article	
planet		tiny	
tidy		planet	
article		belong	
exclaim		molecule	
tidy		roar	
belong		popular	
tiny		direct	
planet		tidy	
article		exclaim	
direct		belong	
molecule		molecule	
popular		popular	
roar		tiny	
exclaim		tidy	
tidy		article	
molecule		roar	
roar		direct	
belong		planet	

외우는 게 지루하면 바로 다음 페이지로 넘어가세요!

multitude [mʌ́ltətjùːd]	많은, 다수
brave [breiv]	용감한, 용기
glacier [gléiʃər]	빙하
entitle [intáitl]	자격을 주다, 제목을 붙이다
chemistry [kéməstri]	화학, 궁합
eager [íːgər]	열망, 열심인
suppress [səprés]	억제하다, 억압하다
folk [fouk]	민속의, 민요의
construct [kənstrʌ́kt]	만들다, 건설하다
prohibit [prouhíbit]	금지하다

뜻이 바로 떠오르지 않으면 왼쪽 페이지의 뜻을 보고 적으세요.

multitude		brave	
chemistry		glacier	
eager		prohibit	
brave		suppress	
suppress		construct	
folk		multitude	
prohibit		prohibit	
entitle		suppress	
glacier		construct	
construct		chemistry	
multitude		eager	
eager		entitle	
suppress		brave	
glacier		glacier	
entitle		folk	
chemistry		multitude	
brave		prohibit	
construct		suppress	
folk		construct	
prohibit		chemistry	
multitude		eager	
folk		entitle	
chemistry		brave	
suppress		glacier	
construct		folk	
prohibit		multitude	
glacier		chemistry	
eager		eager	
brave		brave	
entitle		suppress	
multitude		folk	
folk		prohibit	
eager		entitle	
entitle		glacier	
chemistry		construct	

외우는 게 지루하면 바로 다음 페이지로 넘어가세요!

vertical [və́:rtikəl]	수직의
sweat [swet]	땀을 흘리다
mercy [mə́:rsi]	자비
absurd [æbsə́:rd,]	터무니없는
edge [edʒ]	가장자리, 끝
anticipate [æntísəpèit]	기대하다, 예상하다
moderate [mádərət]	보통의, 중간의
harm [ha:rm]	해치다, 피해를 입히다
jealous [dʒéləs]	질투하는
overhead [ouˈvərheˈd]	위에, 간접적인

뜻이 바로 떠오르지 않으면 왼쪽 페이지의 뜻을 보고 적으세요.

vertical		sweat	
edge		mercy	
anticipate		overhead	
sweat		moderate	
moderate		jealous	
harm		vertical	
overhead		overhead	
absurd		moderate	
mercy		jealous	
jealous		edge	
vertical		anticipate	
anticipate		absurd	
moderate		sweat	
mercy		mercy	
absurd		harm	
edge		vertical	
sweat		overhead	
jealous		moderate	
harm		jealous	
overhead		edge	
vertical		anticipate	
harm		absurd	
edge		sweat	
moderate		mercy	
jealous		harm	
overhead		vertical	
mercy		edge	
anticipate		anticipate	
sweat		sweat	
absurd		moderate	
vertical		harm	
harm		overhead	
anticipate		absurd	
absurd		mercy	
edge		jealous	

외우는 게 지루하면 바로 다음 페이지로 넘어가세요!

surrender [səréndər]	항복하다, 포기하다
flesh [fleʃ]	살, 피부
deserve [dizə́:rv]	자격, 마땅히 ~할 만하다
drain [drein]	배수하다, 유출하다
stiff [stif]	뻣뻣한
survey [sərvéi]	조사하다, 연구하다
cast [kæst]	던지다
cherish [tʃériʃ]	소중히 여기다
peril [pérəl]	위험, 위기
decline [dikláin]	감소하다, 하락하다

surrender		flesh	
stiff		deserve	
survey		decline	
flesh		cast	
cast		peril	
cherish		surrender	
decline		decline	
drain		cast	
deserve		peril	
peril		stiff	
surrender		survey	
survey		drain	
cast		flesh	
deserve		deserve	
drain		cherish	
stiff		surrender	
flesh		decline	
peril		cast	
cherish		peril	
decline		stiff	
surrender		survey	
cherish		drain	
stiff		flesh	
cast		deserve	
peril		cherish	
decline		surrender	
deserve		stiff	
survey		survey	
flesh		flesh	
drain		cast	
surrender		cherish	
cherish		decline	
survey		drain	
drain		deserve	
stiff		peril	

외우는 게 지루하면 바로 다음 페이지로 넘어가세요!

soak [souk]	젖다, 흡수하다
firm [fə:rm]	기업, 회사
philosophy [filásəfi]	철학, 이론
facility [fəsíləti]	시설, 설비
achieve [ətʃí:v]	달성하다, 성취하다
peculiar [pikjú:ljər]	특이한, 특별한
prefer [prifə́:r]	선호하다, 좋아하다
experiment [ikspérəmənt]	실험, 시도
sin [sin]	죄, 죄를 짓다
purchase [pə́:rtʃəs]	구매하다

뜻이 바로 떠오르지 않으면 왼쪽 페이지의 뜻을 보고 적으세요.

soak		firm	
achieve		philosophy	
peculiar		purchase	
firm		prefer	
prefer		sin	
experiment		soak	
purchase		purchase	
facility		prefer	
philosophy		sin	
sin		achieve	
soak		peculiar	
peculiar		facility	
prefer		firm	
philosophy		philosophy	
facility		experiment	
achieve		soak	
firm		purchase	
sin		prefer	
experiment		sin	
purchase		achieve	
soak		peculiar	
experiment		facility	
achieve		firm	
prefer		philosophy	
sin		experiment	
purchase		soak	
philosophy		achieve	
peculiar		peculiar	
firm		firm	
tacility		prefer	
soak		experiment	
experiment		purchase	
peculiar		facility	
facility		philosophy	
achieve		sin	

외우는 게 지루하면 바로 다음 페이지로 넘어가세요!

board [bɔːrd]	위원회, 이사회
tend [tend]	돌보다, 간호하다
environment [inváiərənmənt]	환경, 상황
corps [kɔːr]	단체, 부대
steep [stiːp]	가파른
pleasant [plézənt]	즐거운
zeal [ziːl]	열의, 열기
benefit [bénəfit]	이익, 혜택
attain [ətéin]	달성하다
suburb [sʌbəːrb]	도시 외곽

뜻이 바로 떠오르지 않으면 왼쪽 페이지의 뜻을 보고 적으세요.

board		tend	
steep		environment	
pleasant		suburb	
tend		zeal	
zeal		attain	
benefit		board	
suburb		suburb	
corps		zeal	
environment		attain	
attain		steep	
board		pleasant	
pleasant		corps	
zeal		tend	
environment		environment	
corps		benefit	
steep		board	
tend		suburb	
attain		zeal	
benefit		attain	
suburb		steep	
board		pleasant	
benefit		corps	
steep		tend	
zeal		environment	
attain		benefit	
suburb		board	
environment		steep	
pleasant		pleasant	
tend		tend	
corps		zeal	
board		benefit	
benefit		suburb	
pleasant		corps	
corps		environment	
steep		attain	

외우는 게 지루하면 바로 다음 페이지로 넘어가세요!

anxiety [æŋzáiəti]	불안, 걱정
crucial [krú:ʃəl]	중요한, 결정적인
fold [fould]	접다
royal [rɔ́iəl]	왕실의
envy [énvi]	부러워하다, 질투하다
hostile [hástl]	적대적인, 호전적인
submarine [sʌbməríːn]	잠수함
burst [bəːrst]	터뜨리다
severe [sivíər]	심각한, 무거운
finance [finaéns]	재정, 금융

뜻이 바로 떠오르지 않으면 왼쪽 페이지의 뜻을 보고 적으세요.

anxiety		crucial	
envy		fold	
hostile		finance	
crucial		submarine	
submarine		severe	
burst		anxiety	
finance		finance	
royal		submarine	
fold		severe	
severe		envy	
anxiety		hostile	
hostile		royal	
submarine		crucial	
fold		fold	
royal		burst	
envy		anxiety	
crucial		finance	
severe		submarine	
burst		severe	
finance		envy	
anxiety		hostile	
burst		royal	
envy		crucial	
submarine		fold	
severe		burst	
finance		anxiety	
fold		envy	
hostile		hostile	
crucial		crucial	
royal		submarine	
anxiety		burst	
burst		finance	
hostile		royal	
royal		fold	
envy		severe	

외우는 게 지루하면 바로 다음 페이지로 넘어가세요!

thirst [θəːrst]	갈증, 갈망
otherwise [ʌðərwàiz]	그렇지 않으면
reinforce [rìːinfɔ́ːrs]	보강하다, 강화하다
filter [fíltər]	여과하다
moral [mɔ́ːrəl]	도덕의, 정신적인
precious [préʃəs]	소중한, 귀중한
replace [ripléis]	대체하다, 교제하다
punish [pʌ́niʃ]	처벌하다, 벌주다
arrogant [aérəgənt]	오만한, 거만한
pause [aérəgənt]	멈춤, 휴식

thirst		otherwise	
moral		reinforce	
precious		pause	
otherwise		replace	
replace		arrogant	
punish		thirst	
pause		pause	
filter		replace	
reinforce		arrogant	
arrogant		moral	
thirst		precious	
precious		filter	
replace		otherwise	
reinforce		reinforce	
filter		punish	
moral		thirst	
otherwise		pause	
arrogant		replace	
punish		arrogant	
pause		moral	
thirst		precious	
punish		filter	
moral		otherwise	
replace		reinforce	
arrogant		punish	
pause		thirst	
reinforce		moral	
precious		precious	
otherwise		otherwise	
filter		replace	
thirst		punish	
punish		pause	
precious		filter	
filter		reinforce	
moral		arrogant	

외우는 게 지루하면 바로 다음 페이지로 넘어가세요!

gaze [geiz]	시선, 응시하다
horizon [həráizn]	지평선, 수평선
race [reis]	인종
flat [flæt]	납작한, 평면
organ [ɔ́:rgən]	장기, 기관
loyal [lɔ́iəl]	충성스러운
temper [témpər]	성격, 화
mischief [místʃif]	장난, 악영향
cruel [krú:əl]	잔인한, 잔혹한
convenient [kənví:njənt]	편리한, 간편한

뜻이 바로 떠오르지 않으면 왼쪽 페이지의 뜻을 보고 적으세요.

gaze		horizon	
organ		race	
loyal		convenient	
horizon		temper	
temper		cruel	
mischief		gaze	
convenient		convenient	
flat		temper	
race		cruel	
cruel		organ	
gaze		loyal	
loyal		flat	
temper		horizon	
race		race	
flat		mischief	
organ		gaze	
horizon		convenient	
cruel		temper	
mischief		cruel	
convenient		organ	
gaze		loyal	
mischief		flat	
organ		horizon	
temper		race	
cruel		mischief	
convenient		gaze	
race		organ	
loyal		loyal	
horizon		horizon	
flat		temper	
gaze		mischief	
mischief		convenient	
loyal		flat	
flat		race	
organ		cruel	

외우는 게 지루하면 바로 다음 페이지로 넘어가세요!

undergo [əˌndərgouˈ]	받다, 겪다
tone [toun]	어조, 음조
familiar [fəmíljər]	익숙한, 친숙한
establish [istaébliʃ]	설립하다, 세우다
random [raéndəm]	무작위
patriot [péitriət]	애국자
region [ríːdʒən]	지역, 지방
population [pápjuléiʃən]	인구, 사람들
urgent [ə́ːrdʒənt]	긴급한, 급박한
attract [ətraékt]	끌다, 유혹하다

뜻이 바로 떠오르지 않으면 왼쪽 페이지의 뜻을 보고 적으세요.

undergo		tone	
random		familiar	
patriot		attract	
tone		region	
region		urgent	
population		undergo	
attract		attract	
establish		region	
familiar		urgent	
urgent		random	
undergo		patriot	
patriot		establish	
region		tone	
familiar		familiar	
establish		population	
random		undergo	
tone		attract	
urgent		region	
population		urgent	
attract		random	
undergo		patriot	
population		establish	
random		tone	
region		familiar	
urgent		population	
attract		undergo	
familiar		random	
patriot		patriot	
tone		tone	
establish		region	
undergo		population	
population		attract	
patriot		establish	
establish		familiar	
random		urgent	

외우는 게 지루하면 바로 다음 페이지로 넘어가세요!

destruction [distrʌ́kʃən]	파괴, 파멸
penalty [pénəlti]	처벌, 벌금, 불이익
detect [ditékt]	찾아내다
stimulate [stímjulèit]	자극하다, 촉진시키다
pronounce [prənáuns]	발음하다, 두드러지다
interrupt [ìntərʌ́pt]	방해하다
physics [fíziks]	물리학
trust [trʌst]	신뢰, 믿음
pupil [pjúːpl]	학생, 제자
certificate [sərtífikeit]	증서, 자격증

뜻이 바로 떠오르지 않으면 왼쪽 페이지의 뜻을 보고 적으세요.

destruction		penalty	
pronounce		detect	
interrupt		certificate	
penalty		physics	
physics		pupil	
trust		destruction	
certificate		certificate	
stimulate		physics	
detect		pupil	
pupil		pronounce	
destruction		interrupt	
interrupt		stimulate	
physics		penalty	
detect		detect	
stimulate		trust	
pronounce		destruction	
penalty		certificate	
pupil		physics	
trust		pupil	
certificate		pronounce	
destruction		interrupt	
trust		stimulate	
pronounce		penalty	
physics		detect	
pupil		trust	
certificate		destruction	
detect		pronounce	
interrupt		interrupt	
penalty		penalty	
stimulate		physics	
destruction		trust	
trust		certificate	
interrupt		stimulate	
stimulate		detect	
pronounce		pupil	

외우는 게 지루하면 바로 다음 페이지로 넘어가세요!

fund [fʌnd]	자금, 투자하다
deny [dinái]	부인하다, 부정하다
frame [freim]	구조, 틀
desert [dézərt]	버리다, 비우다
sigh [sai]	한숨
amaze [əméiz]	놀랍다, 멋진
extreme [ikstríːm]	극단적인, 극심한
bind [baind]	결합하다, 구속되다
withdraw [wiðdrɔ́ː]	철수하다, 철회하다
pure [pjuər]	순수한, 순전한

fund		deny	
sigh		frame	
amaze		pure	
deny		extreme	
extreme		withdraw	
bind		fund	
pure		pure	
desert		extreme	
frame		withdraw	
withdraw		sigh	
fund		amaze	
amaze		desert	
extreme		deny	
frame		frame	
desert		bind	
sigh		fund	
deny		pure	
withdraw		extreme	
bind		withdraw	
pure		sigh	
fund		amaze	
bind		desert	
sigh		deny	
extreme		frame	
withdraw		bind	
pure		fund	
frame		sigh	
amaze		amaze	
deny		deny	
desert		extreme	
fund		bind	
bind		pure	
amaze		desert	
desert		frame	
sigh		withdraw	

discourage [diskə́:ridʒ]	낙담시키다, 단념시키다
strict [strikt]	엄격한, 강력한
demonstrate [démənstrèit]	증명하다, 시위하다
upset [ʌpset]	화난, 기분 나쁜
separate [sépərèit]	분리하다, 개별적인
thermometer [θəˈmɒmɪtə(r)]	온도계
alike [əláik]	똑같이, 모두, 비슷한
dawn [dɔ:n]	새벽
warrior [wɔ́:riər]	전사, 병사
drift [drift]	떠다니다, 멀어지다

뜻이 바로 떠오르지 않으면 왼쪽 페이지의 뜻을 보고 적으세요.

discourage		strict	
separate		demonstrate	
thermometer		drift	
strict		alike	
alike		warrior	
dawn		discourage	
drift		drift	
upset		alike	
demonstrate		warrior	
warrior		separate	
discourage		thermometer	
thermometer		upset	
alike		strict	
demonstrate		demonstrate	
upset		dawn	
separate		discourage	
strict		drift	
warrior		alike	
dawn		warrior	
drift		separate	
discourage		thermometer	
dawn		upset	
separate		strict	
alike		demonstrate	
warrior		dawn	
drift		discourage	
demonstrate		separate	
thermometer		thermometer	
strict		strict	
upset		alike	
discourage		dawn	
dawn		drift	
thermometer		upset	
upset		demonstrate	
separate		warrior	

외우는 게 지루하면 바로 다음 페이지로 넘어가세요!

convey [kənvéi]	전달하다, 전하다
indicate [índikèit]	가리키다, 지적하다
phase [feiz]	단계, 상태
summon [sʌmən]	소환하다, 불러내다
remedy [rémədi]	구제하다, 치료하다
deliver [dilívər]	전달하다, 배달하다
subtle [sʌtl]	미묘한, 섬세한
industry [índəstri]	산업, 업계
warn [wɔːrn]	경고하다, 주의하다
sow [sou]	뿌리다

뜻이 바로 떠오르지 않으면 왼쪽 페이지의 뜻을 보고 적으세요.

convey		indicate	
remedy		phase	
deliver		sow	
indicate		subtle	
subtle		warn	
industry		convey	
sow		sow	
summon		subtle	
phase		warn	
warn		remedy	
convey		deliver	
deliver		summon	
subtle		indicate	
phase		phase	
summon		industry	
remedy		convey	
indicate		sow	
warn		subtle	
industry		warn	
sow		remedy	
convey		deliver	
industry		summon	
remedy		indicate	
subtle		phase	
warn		industry	
sow		convey	
phase		remedy	
deliver		deliver	
indicate		indicate	
summon		subtle	
convey		industry	
industry		sow	
deliver		summon	
summon		phase	
remedy		warn	

외우는 게 지루하면 바로 다음 페이지로 넘어가세요!

progress [prágres]	발전, 진전
opinion [əpínjən]	의견, 여론
monument [mánjumənt]	기념물, 유적
breed [briːd]	품종, 육성
debt [det]	부채, 빚
elect [ilékt]	선출된, 당선자
exchange [ikstʃéindʒ]	교환, 교환하다
access [aékses]	접근, 이용
basis [béisis]	기초, 근거
infect [infékt]	감염시키다, 오염시키다

뜻이 바로 떠오르지 않으면 왼쪽 페이지의 뜻을 보고 적으세요.

progress		opinion	
debt		monument	
elect		infect	
opinion		exchange	
exchange		basis	
access		progress	
infect		infect	
breed		exchange	
monument		basis	
basis		debt	
progress		elect	
elect		breed	
exchange		opinion	
monument		monument	
breed		access	
debt		progress	
opinion		infect	
basis		exchange	
access		basis	
infect		debt	
progress		elect	
access		breed	
debt		opinion	
exchange		monument	
basis		access	
infect		progress	
monument		debt	
elect		elect	
opinion		opinion	
breed		exchange	
progress		access	
access		infect	
elect		breed	
breed		monument	
debt		basis	

외우는 게 지루하면 바로 다음 페이지로 넘어가세요!

profit [práfit]	이익, 수익
request [rikwést]	요청, 요구
conscience [kánʃəns]	양심, 의식
meadow [médou]	목초지, 초원
audience [ɔ́ːdiəns]	관객, 청중
specific [spisífik]	특정한, 구체적인
accompany [əkʌ́mpəni]	동행하다, 함께하다
blend [blend]	혼합, 혼합물
devise [diváiz]	고안하다, 마련하다
regard [rigáːrd]	관련되다, 간주하다

profit	request
audience	conscience
specific	regard
request	accompany
accompany	devise
blend	profit
regard	regard
meadow	accompany
conscience	devise
devise	audience
profit	specific
specific	meadow
accompany	request
conscience	conscience
meadow	blend
audience	profit
request	regard
devise	accompany
blend	devise
regard	audience
profit	specific
blend	meadow
audience	request
accompany	conscience
devise	blend
regard	profit
conscience	audience
specific	specific
request	request
meadow	accompany
profit	blend
blend	regard
specific	meadow
meadow	conscience
audience	devise

외우는 게 지루하면 바로 다음 페이지로 넘어가세요!

tempt [tempt]	유혹하다
conceal [kənsíːl]	감추다, 숨기다
vote [vout]	투표하다, 투표
cope [koup]	대처하다, 맞서다
command [kəmaénd]	명령하다, 사령부
significant [signífikənt]	중요한, 상당한
tease [tiːz]	놀리다, 괴롭히다
rank [ræŋk]	차지하다, 오르다
dedicate [dédikèit]	헌신하다, 바치다
sufficient [səfíʃənt]	충분한, 만족스러운

뜻이 바로 떠오르지 않으면 왼쪽 페이지의 뜻을 보고 적으세요.

tempt		conceal	
command		vote	
significant		sufficient	
conceal		tease	
tease		dedicate	
rank		tempt	
sufficient		sufficient	
cope		tease	
vote		dedicate	
dedicate		command	
tempt		significant	
significant		cope	
tease		conceal	
vote		vote	
cope		rank	
command		tempt	
conceal		sufficient	
dedicate		tease	
rank		dedicate	
sufficient		command	
tempt		significant	
rank		cope	
command		conceal	
tease		vote	
dedicate		rank	
sufficient		tempt	
vote		command	
significant		significant	
conceal		conceal	
cope		tease	
tempt		rank	
rank		sufficient	
significant		cope	
cope		vote	
command		dedicate	

외우는 게 지루하면 바로 다음 페이지로 넘어가세요!

account [əkáunt]	계좌, 간주하다
effect [ifékt]	영향, 효과
permanent [pə́:rmənənt]	영구적인
revolt [rivóult]	반란, 저항
triumph [tráiəmf]	승리, 이기다
metropolis [mitrápəlis]	대도시
exquisite [ikskwízit]	정교한, 절묘한
apply [əplái]	적용하다, 지원하다
adapt [ədaépt]	적응하다, 변화
regulate [régjulèit]	규제하다

account		effect	
triumph		permanent	
metropolis		regulate	
effect		exquisite	
exquisite		adapt	
apply		account	
regulate		regulate	
revolt		exquisite	
permanent		adapt	
adapt		triumph	
account		metropolis	
metropolis		revolt	
exquisite		effect	
permanent		permanent	
revolt		apply	
triumph		account	
effect		regulate	
adapt		exquisite	
apply		adapt	
regulate		triumph	
account		metropolis	
apply		revolt	
triumph		effect	
exquisite		permanent	
adapt		apply	
regulate		account	
permanent		triumph	
metropolis		metropolis	
effect		effcct	
revolt		exquisite	
account		apply	
apply		regulate	
metropolis		revolt	
revolt		permanent	
triumph		adapt	

외우는 게 지루하면 바로 다음 페이지로 넘어가세요!

lose [luːz]	잃다, 지다
oblige [əbláidʒ]	~에게 강요하다
advantage [ædvaéntidʒ]	이점, 장점
disturb [distə́ːrb]	방해하다, 건드리다
mean [miːn]	~을 뜻하다
boundary [báundəri]	경계, 영역
communism [kámjunìzm]	공산주의
plain [plein]	평원, 분명한
enclose [inklóuz]	에워싸다, 둘러싸다
astonish [əstániʃ]	놀라운, 놀라게 하다

뜻이 바로 떠오르지 않으면 왼쪽 페이지의 뜻을 보고 적으세요.

lose	oblige
mean	advantage
boundary	astonish
oblige	communism
communism	enclose
plain	lose
astonish	astonish
disturb	communism
advantage	enclose
enclose	mean
lose	boundary
boundary	disturb
communism	oblige
advantage	advantage
disturb	plain
mean	lose
oblige	astonish
enclose	communism
plain	enclose
astonish	mean
lose	boundary
plain	disturb
mean	oblige
communism	advantage
enclose	plain
astonish	lose
advantage	mean
boundary	boundary
oblige	oblige
disturb	communism
lose	plain
plain	astonish
boundary	disturb
disturb	advantage
mean	enclose

외우는 게 지루하면 바로 다음 페이지로 넘어가세요!

fragile [fraédʒəl]	취약한, 깨지기 쉬운
realize [ríːəlàiz]	깨닫다, 알다
patience [péiʃəns]	인내, 참을성
delicious [dilíʃəs]	맛있는
resemble [rizémbl]	닮다, 유사하다
postscript [póustskrìpt]	추신, 후기
outcome [auˈtkəˌm]	결과, 성과
inquire [inkwáiər]	문의하다, 조사하다
exclude [iksklúːd]	제외하다, 배제하다
vague [veig]	모호한, 애매한

뜻이 바로 떠오르지 않으면 왼쪽 페이지의 뜻을 보고 적으세요.

fragile		realize	
resemble		patience	
postscript		vague	
realize		outcome	
outcome		exclude	
inquire		fragile	
vague		vague	
delicious		outcome	
patience		exclude	
exclude		resemble	
fragile		postscript	
postscript		delicious	
outcome		realize	
patience		patience	
delicious		inquire	
resemble		fragile	
realize		vague	
exclude		outcome	
inquire		exclude	
vague		resemble	
fragile		postscript	
inquire		delicious	
resemble		realize	
outcome		patience	
exclude		inquire	
vague		fragile	
patience		resemble	
postscript		postscript	
realize		realize	
delicious		outcome	
fragile		inquire	
inquire		vague	
postscript		delicious	
delicious		patience	
resemble		exclude	

외우는 게 지루하면 바로 다음 페이지로 넘어가세요!

differ [dífər]	다르다, 차이
emotion [imóuʃən]	감정, 정서
classic [klaésik]	고전의, 클래식
bond [band]	채권, 결속
simultaneous [sàiməltéiniəs]	동시의, 동반의
blame [bleim]	비난하다
contradict [kántrədíkt]	모순되다, 다르다
bliss [blis]	행복
encourage [inkə́ːridʒ]	격려하다, 장려하다
add [æd]	덧붙이다, 더하다

뜻이 바로 떠오르지 않으면 왼쪽 페이지의 뜻을 보고 적으세요.

differ		emotion	
simultaneous		classic	
blame		add	
emotion		contradict	
contradict		encourage	
bliss		differ	
add		add	
bond		contradict	
classic		encourage	
encourage		simultaneous	
differ		blame	
blame		bond	
contradict		emotion	
classic		classic	
bond		bliss	
simultaneous		differ	
emotion		add	
encourage		contradict	
bliss		encourage	
add		simultaneous	
differ		blame	
bliss		bond	
simultaneous		emotion	
contradict		classic	
encourage		bliss	
add		differ	
classic		simultaneous	
blame		blame	
emotion		emotion	
bond		contradict	
differ		bliss	
bliss		add	
blame		bond	
bond		classic	
simultaneous		encourage	

외우는 게 지루하면 바로 다음 페이지로 넘어가세요!

decent [díːsnt]	제대로 된, 품위 있는
conquer [káŋkər]	정복하다, 차지하다
politics [pá`lətìks]	정치, 정계
flatter [flaétər]	아첨하다, 납작해지다
aircraft [e'rkræ`ft]	항공기, 비행기
commerce [káməːrs]	상업, 무역
settle [sétl]	해결하다, 정착하다
qualify [kwáləfài]	자격을 얻다
crash [kræʃ]	충돌하다, 추락하다
institute [ínstətjùːt]	연구소, 전문 교육 기관

뜻이 바로 떠오르지 않으면 왼쪽 페이지의 뜻을 보고 적으세요.

decent		conquer	
aircraft		politics	
commerce		institute	
conquer		settle	
settle		crash	
qualify		decent	
institute		institute	
flatter		settle	
politics		crash	
crash		aircraft	
decent		commerce	
commerce		flatter	
settle		conquer	
politics		politics	
flatter		qualify	
aircraft		decent	
conquer		institute	
crash		settle	
qualify		crash	
institute		aircraft	
decent		commerce	
qualify		flatter	
aircraft		conquer	
settle		politics	
crash		qualify	
institute		decent	
politics		aircraft	
commerce		commerce	
conquer		conquer	
flatter		settle	
decent		qualify	
qualify		institute	
commerce		flatter	
flatter		politics	
aircraft		crash	

외우는 게 지루하면 바로 다음 페이지로 넘어가세요!

futile [fjú:tl]	헛된, 헛수고
grand [grǽnd]	웅장한, 위대한
pollute [pəlú:t]	오염시키다
strategy [strǽtədʒi]	전략, 방법
evaluate [ivǽljuèit]	평가하다, 측정하다
cancel [kǽnsəl]	취소하다, 철회하다
cause [kɔːz]	원인, 초래하다
supreme [səprí:m]	최고의, 최상의
juvenile [dʒú:vənl]	청소년의
deprive [dipráiv]	박탈하다, 빼앗다

뜻이 바로 떠오르지 않으면 왼쪽 페이지의 뜻을 보고 적으세요.

futile		grand	
evaluate		pollute	
cancel		deprive	
grand		cause	
cause		juvenile	
supreme		futile	
deprive		deprive	
strategy		cause	
pollute		juvenile	
juvenile		evaluate	
futile		cancel	
cancel		strategy	
cause		grand	
pollute		pollute	
strategy		supreme	
evaluate		futile	
grand		deprive	
juvenile		cause	
supreme		juvenile	
deprive		evaluate	
futile		cancel	
supreme		strategy	
evaluate		grand	
cause		pollute	
juvenile		supreme	
deprive		futile	
pollute		evaluate	
cancel		cancel	
grand		grand	
strategy		cause	
futile		supreme	
supreme		deprive	
cancel		strategy	
strategy		pollute	
evaluate		juvenile	

외우는 게 지루하면 바로 다음 페이지로 넘어가세요!

insult [insʌ́lt]	모욕하다, 욕보이다
explore [iksplɔ́ːr]	탐구하다, 탐험하다
mass [mæs]	대중의
discard [diská:rd]	버리다
suspend [səspénd]	중단하다, 정지하다
statistics [stətístiks]	통계학
sympathy [símpəθi]	공감
available [əvéiləbl]	가능한, 이용할 수 있는
respect [rispékt]	존중, 존경하다
preface [préfis]	서문

뜻이 바로 떠오르지 않으면 왼쪽 페이지의 뜻을 보고 적으세요.

insult		explore	
suspend		mass	
statistics		preface	
explore		sympathy	
sympathy		respect	
available		insult	
preface		preface	
discard		sympathy	
mass		respect	
respect		suspend	
insult		statistics	
statistics		discard	
sympathy		explore	
mass		mass	
discard		available	
suspend		insult	
explore		preface	
respect		sympathy	
available		respect	
preface		suspend	
insult		statistics	
available		discard	
suspend		explore	
sympathy		mass	
respect		available	
preface		insult	
mass		suspend	
statistics		statistics	
explore		explore	
discard		sympathy	
insult		available	
available		preface	
statistics		discard	
discard		mass	
suspend		respect	

외우는 게 지루하면 바로 다음 페이지로 넘어가세요!

conflict [kənflíkt]	갈등, 분쟁
precede [prisí:d]	앞서다, 선행하다
extent [ikstént]	정도, 범위
witness [wítnis]	보다, 목격자
inflict [inflíkt]	주다, 가하다
complain [kəmpléin]	불평하다
multiply [mʌltəplài]	곱하다, 늘리다
neutral [njú:trəl]	중립, 중성
eternal [njú:trəl]	영원한, 불멸의
donate [dóuneit]	기부하다, 기증하다

뜻이 바로 떠오르지 않으면 왼쪽 페이지의 뜻을 보고 적으세요.

conflict		precede	
inflict		extent	
complain		donate	
precede		multiply	
multiply		eternal	
neutral		conflict	
donate		donate	
witness		multiply	
extent		eternal	
eternal		inflict	
conflict		complain	
complain		witness	
multiply		precede	
extent		extent	
witness		neutral	
inflict		conflict	
precede		donate	
eternal		multiply	
neutral		eternal	
donate		inflict	
conflict		complain	
neutral		witness	
inflict		precede	
multiply		extent	
eternal		neutral	
donate		conflict	
extent		inflict	
complain		complain	
precede		precede	
witness		multiply	
conflict		neutral	
neutral		donate	
complain		witness	
witness		extent	
inflict		eternal	

inform [infɔ́:rm]	알리다, 통보하다
remark [rimá:rk]	발언, 말
warrant [wɔ́:rənt]	(체포, 구속) 영장
solemn [sáləm]	엄숙한, 진지한
souvenir [sù:vəníər]	기념품
range [reindʒ]	범위, 영역
spill [spil]	유출, 쏟다
vacant [véikənt]	공석인, 텅빈
apparent [əpaérənt]	분명한, 명백한
conclude [kənklú:d]	결론짓다, 체결하다

뜻이 바로 떠오르지 않으면 왼쪽 페이지의 뜻을 보고 적으세요.

inform		remark	
souvenir		warrant	
range		conclude	
remark		spill	
spill		apparent	
vacant		inform	
conclude		conclude	
solemn		spill	
warrant		apparent	
apparent		souvenir	
inform		range	
range		solemn	
spill		remark	
warrant		warrant	
solemn		vacant	
souvenir		inform	
remark		conclude	
apparent		spill	
vacant		apparent	
conclude		souvenir	
inform		range	
vacant		solemn	
souvenir		remark	
spill		warrant	
apparent		vacant	
conclude		inform	
warrant		souvenir	
range		range	
remark		remark	
solemn		spill	
inform		vacant	
vacant		conclude	
range		solemn	
solemn		warrant	
souvenir		apparent	

외우는 게 지루하면 바로 다음 페이지로 넘어가세요!

violence [váiələns]	폭력, 범죄
personality [pə̀:rsənaéləti]	개성, 인성
definite [défənit]	명확한, 분명한
represent [rèprizént]	대표하다, 나타내다
affection [əfékʃən]	애정, 애착
recollect [rèkəlékt]	회상하다, 생각나다
literature [lítərətʃər]	문학, 문예
chop [tʃɑp]	자르다, 베다
shield [ʃi:ld]	방패, 보호하다
respond [rispánd]	반응하다, 대응하다

뜻이 바로 떠오르지 않으면 왼쪽 페이지의 뜻을 보고 적으세요.

violence		personality	
affection		definite	
recollect		respond	
personality		literature	
literature		shield	
chop		violence	
respond		respond	
represent		literature	
definite		shield	
shield		affection	
violence		recollect	
recollect		represent	
literature		personality	
definite		definite	
represent		chop	
affection		violence	
personality		respond	
shield		literature	
chop		shield	
respond		affection	
violence		recollect	
chop		represent	
affection		personality	
literature		definite	
shield		chop	
respond		violence	
definite		affection	
recollect		recollect	
personality		personality	
represent		literature	
violence		chop	
chop		respond	
recollect		represent	
represent		definite	
affection		shield	

외우는 게 지루하면 바로 다음 페이지로 넘어가세요!

generate [dʒénərèit]	생성하다
impress [imprés]	인상, 감동시키다
barn [ba:rn]	외양간, 헛간
effective [iféktiv]	효과적인, 효율적인
essential [isénʃəl]	필수의, 필요한
amuse [əmjúːz]	재미있게 하다, 즐겁게 하다
autograph [ɔ́ːtəgræ̀f]	서명, 서명하다
celebrity [səlébrəti]	유명인, 연예인
scratch [skrætʃ]	긁다, 스크래치
regret [rigrét]	후회하다, 유감

뜻이 바로 떠오르지 않으면 왼쪽 페이지의 뜻을 보고 적으세요.

generate		impress	
essential		barn	
amuse		regret	
impress		autograph	
autograph		scratch	
celebrity		generate	
regret		regret	
effective		autograph	
barn		scratch	
scratch		essential	
generate		amuse	
amuse		effective	
autograph		impress	
barn		barn	
effective		celebrity	
essential		generate	
impress		regret	
scratch		autograph	
celebrity		scratch	
regret		essential	
generate		amuse	
celebrity		effective	
essential		impress	
autograph		barn	
scratch		celebrity	
regret		generate	
barn		essential	
amuse		amuse	
impress		impress	
effective		autograph	
generate		celebrity	
celebrity		regret	
amuse		effective	
effective		barn	
essential		scratch	

외우는 게 지루하면 바로 다음 페이지로 넘어가세요!

vehicle [víːikl]	탈 것, 운송 수단
hardship [háːrdʃip]	고난, 어려움
weigh [wei]	무게가 나가다, 압박하다
privilege [prívəlidʒ]	특권
shortage [ʃɔ́ːrtidʒ]	부족, 결핍
vast [væst]	광대한, 거대한
immense [iméns]	굉장한, 막대한
route [ruːt, raut]	길, 방법
pace [peis]	속도, 페이스
weep [wiːp]	눈물을 흘리다

뜻이 바로 떠오르지 않으면 왼쪽 페이지의 뜻을 보고 적으세요.

vehicle		hardship	
shortage		weigh	
vast		weep	
hardship		immense	
immense		pace	
route		vehicle	
weep		weep	
privilege		immense	
weigh		pace	
pace		shortage	
vehicle		vast	
vast		privilege	
immense		hardship	
weigh		weigh	
privilege		route	
shortage		vehicle	
hardship		weep	
pace		immense	
route		pace	
weep		shortage	
vehicle		vast	
route		privilege	
shortage		hardship	
immense		weigh	
pace		route	
weep		vehicle	
weigh		shortage	
vast		vast	
hardship		hardship	
privilege		immense	
vehicle		route	
route		weep	
vast		privilege	
privilege		weigh	
shortage		pace	

외우는 게 지루하면 바로 다음 페이지로 넘어가세요!

responsible [rispánsəbl]	책임이 있는
examine [igzaémin]	조사하다, 검토하다
interpret [intə́:rprit]	해석하다, 통역하다
counterpart [káuntərpá:rt]	상대방
vary [véəri]	다양하다
admit [ædmít]	인정하다, 시인하다
evolution [èvəlú:ʃən]	진화, 변화
register [rédʒistər]	등록하다, 기록하다
fee [fi:]	요금, 금액
enthusiasm [inθú:ziæzm]	열정, 열광

뜻이 바로 떠오르지 않으면 왼쪽 페이지의 뜻을 보고 적으세요.

responsible		examine	
vary		interpret	
admit		enthusiasm	
examine		evolution	
evolution		fee	
register		responsible	
enthusiasm		enthusiasm	
counterpart		evolution	
interpret		fee	
fee		vary	
responsible		admit	
admit		counterpart	
evolution		examine	
interpret		interpret	
counterpart		register	
vary		responsible	
examine		enthusiasm	
fee		evolution	
register		fee	
enthusiasm		vary	
responsible		admit	
register		counterpart	
vary		examine	
evolution		interpret	
fee		register	
enthusiasm		responsible	
interpret		vary	
admit		admit	
examine		examine	
counterpart		evolution	
responsible		register	
register		enthusiasm	
admit		counterpart	
counterpart		interpret	
vary		fee	

외우는 게 지루하면 바로 다음 페이지로 넘어가세요!

statue [staétʃuː]	동상
flavor [fléivər]	맛, 향
illustrate [íləstrèit]	설명하다, 삽화를 넣다
behavior [bihéivjər]	행동, 행위
procedure [prəsíːdʒər]	절차, 과정
avenge [əvéndʒ]	복수하다
descend [disénd]	내려오다
incredible [inkrédəbl]	엄청난, 놀라운
ripe [raip]	잘 익은
justify [dʒʌstəfài]	정당화하다

뜻이 바로 떠오르지 않으면 왼쪽 페이지의 뜻을 보고 적으세요.

statue		flavor	
procedure		illustrate	
avenge		justify	
flavor		descend	
descend		ripe	
incredible		statue	
justify		justify	
behavior		descend	
illustrate		ripe	
ripe		procedure	
statue		avenge	
avenge		behavior	
descend		flavor	
illustrate		illustrate	
behavior		incredible	
procedure		statue	
flavor		justify	
ripe		descend	
incredible		ripe	
justify		procedure	
statue		avenge	
incredible		behavior	
procedure		flavor	
descend		illustrate	
ripe		incredible	
justify		statue	
illustrate		procedure	
avenge		avenge	
flavor		flavor	
behavior		descend	
statue		incredible	
incredible		justify	
avenge		behavior	
behavior		illustrate	
procedure		ripe	

외우는 게 지루하면 바로 다음 페이지로 넘어가세요!

margin [máːrdʒin]	수익
contemporary [kəntémpərèri]	현대의, 최신의
rare [rɛər]	희귀한, 드문
converse [kənvə́ːrs]	대화하다, 이야기하다
confuse [kənfjúːz]	혼동하다
furnish [fə́ːrniʃ]	제공하다, 갖추다
condemn [kəndém]	비난하다, 규탄하다
enable [inéibl]	가능하게 하다
launch [lɔːntʃ]	발사하다, 시작하다
slight [slait]	약간의, 조금

뜻이 바로 떠오르지 않으면 왼쪽 페이지의 뜻을 보고 적으세요.

margin	contemporary
confuse	rare
furnish	slight
contemporary	condemn
condemn	launch
enable	margin
slight	slight
converse	condemn
rare	launch
launch	confuse
margin	furnish
furnish	converse
condemn	contemporary
rare	rare
converse	enable
confuse	margin
contemporary	slight
launch	condemn
enable	launch
slight	confuse
margin	furnish
enable	converse
confuse	contemporary
condemn	rare
launch	enable
slight	margin
rare	confuse
furnish	furnish
contemporary	contemporary
converse	condemn
margin	enable
enable	slight
furnish	converse
converse	rare
confuse	launch

외우는 게 지루하면 바로 다음 페이지로 넘어가세요!

apart [əpá:rt]	떨어진, 분리된
rapid [raépid]	급속한, 빠른
emerge [imə́:rdʒ]	떠오르다, 새로운
export [ikspó:rt]	수출, 수출액
liable [láiəbl]	책임 있는
quit [kwit]	그만두다, 끊다
tender [téndər]	부드러운, 상냥한
brief [bri:f]	보고서, 짧은
reside [rizáid]	거주하다, 살다
impose [impóuz]	부과하다, 제한하다

뜻이 바로 떠오르지 않으면 왼쪽 페이지의 뜻을 보고 적으세요.

apart	rapid	
liable	emerge	
quit	impose	
rapid	tender	
tender	reside	
brief	apart	
impose	impose	
export	tender	
emerge	reside	
reside	liable	
apart	quit	
quit	export	
tender	rapid	
emerge	emerge	
export	brief	
liable	apart	
rapid	impose	
reside	tender	
brief	reside	
impose	liable	
apart	quit	
brief	export	
liable	rapid	
tender	emerge	
reside	brief	
impose	apart	
emerge	liable	
quit	quit	
rapid	rapid	
export	tender	
apart	brief	
brief	impose	
quit	export	
export	emerge	
liable	reside	

외우는 게 지루하면 바로 다음 페이지로 넘어가세요!

harsh [ha:rʃ]	가혹한, 거친
session [séʃən]	회의, 회기
confirm [kənfə́:rm]	확인하다, 확정하다
faculty [faékəlti]	능력
pray [prei]	기도하다, 기원하다
transform [trænsfɔ́'rm]	바꾸어 놓다, 변화시키다
historic [histɔ́:rik]	역사적인
diameter [daiaémətər]	직경, 지름
geology [dʒiálədʒi]	지질학
revise [riváiz]	개정하다, 수정하다

뜻이 바로 떠오르지 않으면 왼쪽 페이지의 뜻을 보고 적으세요.

harsh	session	
pray	confirm	
transform	revise	
session	historic	
historic	geology	
diameter	harsh	
revise	revise	
faculty	historic	
confirm	geology	
geology	pray	
harsh	transform	
transform	faculty	
historic	session	
confirm	confirm	
faculty	diameter	
pray	harsh	
session	revise	
geology	historic	
diameter	geology	
revise	pray	
harsh	transform	
diameter	faculty	
pray	session	
historic	confirm	
geology	diameter	
revise	harsh	
confirm	pray	
transform	transform	
session	session	
faculty	historic	
harsh	diameter	
diameter	revise	
transform	faculty	
faculty	confirm	
pray	geology	

confident [kánfədənt]	자신 있는, 확신하는
distract [distraékt]	주의를 빼앗다
fellow [félou]	동료, 연구원
hazard [haézərd]	위험, 해이
disaster [dizaéstər]	재난, 재앙
disclose [disklóuz]	공개하다, 밝히다
obtain [əbtéin]	얻다, 입수하다
calm [ka:m]	차분한, 진정시키다
appoint [əpɔ́int]	임명하다, 지명하다
contend [kənténd]	주장하다, 싸우다

뜻이 바로 떠오르지 않으면 왼쪽 페이지의 뜻을 보고 적으세요.

confident		distract	
disaster		fellow	
disclose		contend	
distract		obtain	
obtain		appoint	
calm		confident	
contend		contend	
hazard		obtain	
fellow		appoint	
appoint		disaster	
confident		disclose	
disclose		hazard	
obtain		distract	
fellow		fellow	
hazard		calm	
disaster		confident	
distract		contend	
appoint		obtain	
calm		appoint	
contend		disaster	
confident		disclose	
calm		hazard	
disaster		distract	
obtain		fellow	
appoint		calm	
contend		confident	
fellow		disaster	
disclose		disclose	
distract		distract	
hazard		obtain	
confident		calm	
calm		contend	
disclose		hazard	
hazard		fellow	
disaster		appoint	

외우는 게 지루하면 바로 다음 페이지로 넘어가세요!

inherent [inhíərənt]	내재된, 고유의
broadcast [brɔ́ːdkæst]	방송하다, 방영하다
dwell [dwel]	살다, 생각하다
remind [rimáind]	알려 주다, 상기시키다
bullet [búlit]	총알, 총탄
distribute [distríbjuːt]	나눠 주다, 배포하다
shy [ʃai]	수줍은, 부끄러운
material [mətíəriəl]	물질의, 재료
urge [əːrdʒ]	촉구하다, 요구하다
structure [strʌ́ktʃər]	구조, 구성하다

뜻이 바로 떠오르지 않으면 왼쪽 페이지의 뜻을 보고 적으세요.

inherent		broadcast	
bullet		dwell	
distribute		structure	
broadcast		shy	
shy		urge	
material		inherent	
structure		structure	
remind		shy	
dwell		urge	
urge		bullet	
inherent		distribute	
distribute		remind	
shy		broadcast	
dwell		dwell	
remind		material	
bullet		inherent	
broadcast		structure	
urge		shy	
material		urge	
structure		bullet	
inherent		distribute	
material		remind	
bullet		broadcast	
shy		dwell	
urge		material	
structure		inherent	
dwell		bullet	
distribute		distribute	
broadcast		broadcast	
remind		shy	
inherent		material	
material		structure	
distribute		remind	
remind		dwell	
bullet		urge	

assemble [əsémbl]	조립하다, 모으다
disappoint [dìsəpɔ́int]	실망시키다, 낙담시키다
predict [pridíkt]	예측하다, 전망하다
proceed [prəsí:d]	진행하다, 계속하다
civil [sívəl]	시민의, 민간의
escape [iskéip]	탈출하다, 벗어나다
row [rou]	(옆으로 늘어선) 줄
parallel [pǽrəlèl]	평행, 유사
clue [klu:]	단서, 실마리
string [striŋ]	줄, 현악

뜻이 바로 떠오르지 않으면 왼쪽 페이지의 뜻을 보고 적으세요.

assemble		disappoint	
civil		predict	
escape		string	
disappoint		row	
row		clue	
parallel		assemble	
string		string	
proceed		row	
predict		clue	
clue		civil	
assemble		escape	
escape		proceed	
row		disappoint	
predict		predict	
proceed		parallel	
civil		assemble	
disappoint		string	
clue		row	
parallel		clue	
string		civil	
assemble		escape	
parallel		proceed	
civil		disappoint	
row		predict	
clue		parallel	
string		assemble	
predict		civil	
escape		escape	
disappoint		disappoint	
proceed		row	
assemble		parallel	
parallel		string	
escape		proceed	
proceed		predict	
civil		clue	

mutual [mjúːtʃuəl]	서로의
fuel [fjúːəl]	연료
insight [ínsàit]	통찰력
share [ʃɛər]	공유하다, 나누다
lack [læk]	부족, 결핍
publish [pʌ́bliʃ]	출판하다, 발표하다
soil [sɔil]	흙, 땅
display [displéi]	전시하다, 보여 주다
cease [siːs]	중단하다, 사라지다
pose [pouz]	제기하다, 가하다

뜻이 바로 떠오르지 않으면 왼쪽 페이지의 뜻을 보고 적으세요.

mutual		fuel	
lack		insight	
publish		pose	
fuel		soil	
soil		cease	
display		mutual	
pose		pose	
share		soil	
insight		cease	
cease		lack	
mutual		publish	
publish		share	
soil		fuel	
insight		insight	
share		display	
lack		mutual	
fuel		pose	
cease		soil	
display		cease	
pose		lack	
mutual		publish	
display		share	
lack		fuel	
soil		insight	
cease		display	
pose		mutual	
insight		lack	
publish		publish	
fuel		fuel	
share		soil	
mutual		display	
display		pose	
publish		share	
share		insight	
lack		cease	

외우는 게 지루하면 바로 다음 페이지로 넘어가세요!

swear [swɛər]	맹세하다
fiber [fáibər]	섬유, 섬유질
committee [kəmíti]	위원회
initial [iníʃəl]	초기의, 원래의
cabin [kaébin]	객실, 오두막
trace [treis]	추적하다, 흔적
vow [vau]	다짐하다, 천명하다
perceive [pərsíːv]	인지하다, 인식하다
afford [əfɔ́ːrd]	여유가 있다
election [ilékʃən]	선거, 투표

뜻이 바로 떠오르지 않으면 왼쪽 페이지의 뜻을 보고 적으세요.

swear		fiber	
cabin		committee	
trace		election	
fiber		vow	
vow		afford	
perceive		swear	
election		election	
initial		vow	
committee		afford	
afford		cabin	
swear		trace	
trace		initial	
vow		fiber	
committee		committee	
initial		perceive	
cabin		swear	
fiber		election	
afford		vow	
perceive		afford	
election		cabin	
swear		trace	
perceive		initial	
cabin		fiber	
vow		committee	
afford		perceive	
election		swear	
committee		cabin	
trace		trace	
fiber		fiber	
initial		vow	
swear		perceive	
perceive		election	
trace		initial	
initial		committee	
cabin		afford	

determine [ditə́:rmin]	결정하다, 결심하다
found [faund]	발견했다, 찾아냈다
bump [bʌmp]	부딪히다, 마주치다
permit [pərmít]	허가하다, 허용하다
designate [dézignèit]	지정하다, 지명하다
voluntary [válantèri]	자발적인, 자원봉사의
depart [dipá:rt]	떠나다, 출발하다
funeral [fjú:narəl]	장례의, 상례
aisle [ail]	통로, 복도
relate [riléit]	관련시키다, 관계시키다

뜻이 바로 떠오르지 않으면 왼쪽 페이지의 뜻을 보고 적으세요.

determine		found	
designate		bump	
voluntary		relate	
found		depart	
depart		aisle	
funeral		determine	
relate		relate	
permit		depart	
bump		aisle	
aisle		designate	
determine		voluntary	
voluntary		permit	
depart		found	
bump		bump	
permit		funeral	
designate		determine	
found		relate	
aisle		depart	
funeral		aisle	
relate		designate	
determine		voluntary	
funeral		permit	
designate		found	
depart		bump	
aisle		funeral	
relate		determine	
bump		designate	
voluntary		voluntary	
found		found	
permit		depart	
determine		funeral	
funeral		relate	
voluntary		permit	
permit		bump	
designate		aisle	

외우는 게 지루하면 바로 다음 페이지로 넘어가세요!

chief [tʃi:f]	장관, 최고의
confess [kənfés]	고백하다, 자백하다
revolution [rèvəlú:ʃən]	혁명, 혁신
active [aéktiv]	능동적인, 활동적인
besides [bisáidz]	~외에
succeed [səksí:d]	성공하다
mention [ménʃən]	언급하다, 말하다
symptom [símptəm]	증상, 증세
territory [térətɔ̀:ri]	영토, 영역
expose [ikspóuz]	노출하다, 보이다

뜻이 바로 떠오르지 않으면 왼쪽 페이지의 뜻을 보고 적으세요.

chief		confess	
besides		revolution	
succeed		expose	
confess		mention	
mention		territory	
symptom		chief	
expose		expose	
active		mention	
revolution		territory	
territory		besides	
chief		succeed	
succeed		active	
mention		confess	
revolution		revolution	
active		symptom	
besides		chief	
confess		expose	
territory		mention	
symptom		territory	
expose		besides	
chief		succeed	
symptom		active	
besides		confess	
mention		revolution	
territory		symptom	
expose		chief	
revolution		besides	
succeed		succeed	
confess		confess	
active		mention	
chief		symptom	
symptom		expose	
succeed		active	
active		revolution	
besides		territory	

외우는 게 지루하면 바로 다음 페이지로 넘어가세요!

inspire [inspáiər]	영감을 주다, 고무하다
conserve [kənsə́:rv]	~을 보존하다, 보호하다
dispute [dispjú:t]	분쟁, 논쟁
awful [ɔ́:fəl]	끔찍한, 엄청난
horror [hɔ́:rər]	공포, 무서움
courage [kə́:ridʒ]	용기, 용감
withhold [wiðhóuld,]	보류하다, 숨기다
transmit [trænsmít]	전송하다, 전달하다
enforce [infɔ́:rs]	시행하다, 집행하다
rational [ráeʃənl]	합리적인, 이성적인

뜻이 바로 떠오르지 않으면 왼쪽 페이지의 뜻을 보고 적으세요.

inspire		conserve	
horror		dispute	
courage		rational	
conserve		withhold	
withhold		enforce	
transmit		inspire	
rational		rational	
awful		withhold	
dispute		enforce	
enforce		horror	
inspire		courage	
courage		awful	
withhold		conserve	
dispute		dispute	
awful		transmit	
horror		inspire	
conserve		rational	
enforce		withhold	
transmit		enforce	
rational		horror	
inspire		courage	
transmit		awful	
horror		conserve	
withhold		dispute	
enforce		transmit	
rational		inspire	
dispute		horror	
courage		courage	
conserve		conserve	
awful		withhold	
inspire		transmit	
transmit		rational	
courage		awful	
awful		dispute	
horror		enforce	

외우는 게 지루하면 바로 다음 페이지로 넘어가세요!

outlook [auˈtlʊˌk]	전망, 경치
credit [krédit]	신용, 학점
instance [ínstəns]	예, 사례
swift [swift]	신속한, 빠른
imply [implái]	암시하다
helpless [hélplis]	무력한, 속수무책인
discuss [diskʌs]	논의하다, 협의
controversy [kántrəvəːrsi]	논란, 논쟁
release [rilíːs]	발표하다, 개봉하다
curious [kjúəriəs]	궁금한, 알고 싶은

뜻이 바로 떠오르지 않으면 왼쪽 페이지의 뜻을 보고 적으세요.

outlook		credit	
imply		instance	
helpless		curious	
credit		discuss	
discuss		release	
controversy		outlook	
curious		curious	
swift		discuss	
instance		release	
release		imply	
outlook		helpless	
helpless		swift	
discuss		credit	
instance		instance	
swift		controversy	
imply		outlook	
credit		curious	
release		discuss	
controversy		release	
curious		imply	
outlook		helpless	
controversy		swift	
imply		credit	
discuss		instance	
release		controversy	
curious		outlook	
instance		imply	
helpless		helpless	
credit		credit	
swift		discuss	
outlook		controversy	
controversy		curious	
helpless		swift	
swift		instance	
imply		release	

외우는 게 지루하면 바로 다음 페이지로 넘어가세요!

grief [gri:f]	슬픔, 비탄
degree [digrí:]	학위, 등급
gain [gein]	얻다
arrange [əréindʒ]	배치하다, 준비하다
inclined [inkláind]	마음이 내키는, 경향이 있는
cling [kliŋ]	매달리다, 집착하다
delight [diláit]	기쁘게 하다, 기쁘다
faith [feiθ]	신앙, 믿음
rude [ru:d]	무례한, 거친
bold [bould]	힘 있는, 과감한

뜻이 바로 떠오르지 않으면 왼쪽 페이지의 뜻을 보고 적으세요.

grief		degree	
inclined		gain	
cling		bold	
degree		delight	
delight		rude	
faith		grief	
bold		bold	
arrange		delight	
gain		rude	
rude		inclined	
grief		cling	
cling		arrange	
delight		degree	
gain		gain	
arrange		faith	
inclined		grief	
degree		bold	
rude		delight	
faith		rude	
bold		inclined	
grief		cling	
faith		arrange	
inclined		degree	
delight		gain	
rude		faith	
bold		grief	
gain		inclined	
cling		cling	
degree		degree	
arrange		delight	
grief		faith	
faith		bold	
cling		arrange	
arrange		gain	
inclined		rude	

외우는 게 지루하면 바로 다음 페이지로 넘어가세요!

uphold [ʌphóuld]	지키다, 확정하다
fatal [féitl]	치명적인
aid [eid]	지원, 원조
intend [inténd]	의도하다, 계획하다
internal [intə́:rnl]	내부의, 체내의
notice [nóutis]	알아차리다, 주목하다
relieve [rilí:v]	완화시키다, 안도하다
fortune [fɔ́:rtʃən]	재산, 행운
nonsense [nánsens]	말도 안 되는
astronaut [aéstrənɔ̀:t]	우주 비행사

뜻이 바로 떠오르지 않으면 왼쪽 페이지의 뜻을 보고 적으세요.

uphold		fatal	
internal		aid	
notice		astronaut	
fatal		relieve	
relieve		nonsense	
fortune		uphold	
astronaut		astronaut	
intend		relieve	
aid		nonsense	
nonsense		internal	
uphold		notice	
notice		intend	
relieve		fatal	
aid		aid	
intend		fortune	
internal		uphold	
fatal		astronaut	
nonsense		relieve	
fortune		nonsense	
astronaut		internal	
uphold		notice	
fortune		intend	
internal		fatal	
relieve		aid	
nonsense		fortune	
astronaut		uphold	
aid		internal	
notice		notice	
fatal		tatal	
intend		relieve	
uphold		fortune	
fortune		astronaut	
notice		intend	
intend		aid	
internal		nonsense	

paralyze [paérəlàiz]	마비시키다
immune [imjú:n]	면역의, 면제된
equator [ikwéitər]	적도
award [əwɔ́:rd]	상, 수여하다
arrest [ərést]	체포하다, 구속하다
holy [hóuli]	성스러운, 신성한
intellect [íntəlèkt]	지성, 지식인
exist [igzíst]	존재하다, 있다
expert [ékspə:rt]	전문가, 숙련된
greet [gri:t]	인사하다, 맞이하다

뜻이 바로 떠오르지 않으면 왼쪽 페이지의 뜻을 보고 적으세요.

paralyze		immune	
arrest		equator	
holy		greet	
immune		intellect	
intellect		expert	
exist		paralyze	
greet		greet	
award		intellect	
equator		expert	
expert		arrest	
paralyze		holy	
holy		award	
intellect		immune	
equator		equator	
award		exist	
arrest		paralyze	
immune		greet	
expert		intellect	
exist		expert	
greet		arrest	
paralyze		holy	
exist		award	
arrest		immune	
intellect		equator	
expert		exist	
greet		paralyze	
equator		arrest	
holy		holy	
immune		immune	
award		intellect	
paralyze		exist	
exist		greet	
holy		award	
award		equator	
arrest		expert	

외우는 게 지루하면 바로 다음 페이지로 넘어가세요!

declare [dikléər]	선언하다, 말하다
mortal [mɔ́ːrtl]	죽을 운명의, 치명적인
anxious [ǽŋkʃəs]	불안한
hesitate [hézətèit]	망설이다, 주저하다
contact [kántækt]	접촉, 연락
particular [pərtíkjulər]	특정한, 특별한
liberty [líbərti]	자유
participate [paːrtísəpèit]	참여하다, 참가하다
concentrate [kánsəntrèit]	집중시키다, 농축되다
diabetes [dàiəbíːtis]	당뇨병

뜻이 바로 떠오르지 않으면 왼쪽 페이지의 뜻을 보고 적으세요.

declare		mortal	
contact		anxious	
particular		diabetes	
mortal		liberty	
liberty		concentrate	
participate		declare	
diabetes		diabetes	
hesitate		liberty	
anxious		concentrate	
concentrate		contact	
declare		particular	
particular		hesitate	
liberty		mortal	
anxious		anxious	
hesitate		participate	
contact		declare	
mortal		diabetes	
concentrate		liberty	
participate		concentrate	
diabetes		contact	
declare		particular	
participate		hesitate	
contact		mortal	
liberty		anxious	
concentrate		participate	
diabetes		declare	
anxious		contact	
particular		particular	
mortal		mortal	
hesitate		liberty	
declare		participate	
participate		diabetes	
particular		hesitate	
hesitate		anxious	
contact		concentrate	

외우는 게 지루하면 바로 다음 페이지로 넘어가세요!

phenomenon [finámənán]	현상, 장관
fulfill [fulfíl]	이행, 수행
complement [kámpləmənt]	보완하다, 전량
abolish [əbáliʃ]	폐지하다, 없애다
ceiling [síːliŋ]	천장, 한도
decrease [dikríːs]	감소하다, 줄다
meantime [míːntàim]	한편, 그동안
keen [kiːn]	예민한, 예리한
quote [kwout]	인용하다, 전하다
accomplish [əkámpliʃ]	성취하다, 이루다

뜻이 바로 떠오르지 않으면 왼쪽 페이지의 뜻을 보고 적으세요.

phenomenon	fulfill
ceiling	complement
decrease	accomplish
fulfill	meantime
meantime	quote
keen	phenomenon
accomplish	accomplish
abolish	meantime
complement	quote
quote	ceiling
phenomenon	decrease
decrease	abolish
meantime	fulfill
complement	complement
abolish	keen
ceiling	phenomenon
fulfill	accomplish
quote	meantime
keen	quote
accomplish	ceiling
phenomenon	decrease
keen	abolish
ceiling	fulfill
meantime	complement
quote	keen
accomplish	phenomenon
complement	ceiling
decrease	decrease
fulfill	fulfill
abolish	meantime
phenomenon	keen
keen	accomplish
decrease	abolish
abolish	complement
ceiling	quote

외우는 게 지루하면 바로 다음 페이지로 넘어가세요!

resort [rizɔ́ːrt]	리조트, 의존하다
gender [dʒéndər]	성별, 성
sculpture [skʌ́lptʃər]	조각하다, 조각품
breeze [briːz]	바람, 순풍
distinguish [distíŋgwiʃ]	구별하다, 구분하다
conform [kənfɔ́ːrm]	일치하다, 따르다
council [káunsəl]	의회, 위원회
crop [krap]	작물, 농작물
grave [greiv]	무덤
focus [fóukəs]	중심, 집중하다

뜻이 바로 떠오르지 않으면 왼쪽 페이지의 뜻을 보고 적으세요.

resort		gender	
distinguish		sculpture	
conform		focus	
gender		council	
council		grave	
crop		resort	
focus		focus	
breeze		council	
sculpture		grave	
grave		distinguish	
resort		conform	
conform		breeze	
council		gender	
sculpture		sculpture	
breeze		crop	
distinguish		resort	
gender		focus	
grave		council	
crop		grave	
focus		distinguish	
resort		conform	
crop		breeze	
distinguish		gender	
council		sculpture	
grave		crop	
focus		resort	
sculpture		distinguish	
conform		conform	
gender		gender	
breeze		council	
resort		crop	
crop		focus	
conform		breeze	
breeze		sculpture	
distinguish		grave	

외우는 게 지루하면 바로 다음 페이지로 넘어가세요!

remote [rimóut]	원격의, 외딴
ponder [pándər]	숙고하다
dictate [díkteit]	받아쓰게 하다, 지시하다
warehouse [weˈrhauˌs]	창고, 도매점
notion [nóuʃən]	개념, 생각
commercial [kəmə́ːrʃəl]	상업용의, 상업적인
stumble [stʌ́mbl]	비틀거리다
restrain [ristréin]	제한하다, 자제하다
inherit [inhérit]	물려받다, 유전되다
profess [prəfés]	공언하다, 주장하다

remote		ponder	
notion		dictate	
commercial		profess	
ponder		stumble	
stumble		inherit	
restrain		remote	
profess		profess	
warehouse		stumble	
dictate		inherit	
inherit		notion	
remote		commercial	
commercial		warehouse	
stumble		ponder	
dictate		dictate	
warehouse		restrain	
notion		remote	
ponder		profess	
inherit		stumble	
restrain		inherit	
profess		notion	
remote		commercial	
restrain		warehouse	
notion		ponder	
stumble		dictate	
inherit		restrain	
profess		remote	
dictate		notion	
commercial		commercial	
ponder		ponder	
warehouse		stumble	
remote		restrain	
restrain		profess	
commercial		warehouse	
warehouse		dictate	
notion		inherit	

외우는 게 지루하면 바로 다음 페이지로 넘어가세요!

wrap [ræp]	포장하다
signature [sígnətʃər]	서명, 특징
dare [dɛər]	감히 ~ 하다
reproduce [ri͵prədu's]	번식하다, 복제하다
crawl [krɔ:l]	기다, 기어가다
affect [əfékt]	영향을 주다, 작용하다
exhaust [igzɔ́:st]	지치다, 피곤하다
endure [indjúər]	견디다, 지속하다
average [aévəridʒ]	평균, 보통의
alert [ələ́:rt]	경계, 주의하다

뜻이 바로 떠오르지 않으면 왼쪽 페이지의 뜻을 보고 적으세요.

wrap	_____	signature	_____
crawl	_____	dare	_____
affect	_____	alert	_____
signature	_____	exhaust	_____
exhaust	_____	average	_____
endure	_____	wrap	_____
alert	_____	alert	_____
reproduce	_____	exhaust	_____
dare	_____	average	_____
average	_____	crawl	_____
wrap	_____	affect	_____
affect	_____	reproduce	_____
exhaust	_____	signature	_____
dare	_____	dare	_____
reproduce	_____	endure	_____
crawl	_____	wrap	_____
signature	_____	alert	_____
average	_____	exhaust	_____
endure	_____	average	_____
alert	_____	crawl	_____
wrap	_____	affect	_____
endure	_____	reproduce	_____
crawl	_____	signature	_____
exhaust	_____	dare	_____
average	_____	endure	_____
alert	_____	wrap	_____
dare	_____	crawl	_____
affect	_____	affect	_____
signature	_____	signature	_____
reproduce	_____	exhaust	_____
wrap	_____	endure	_____
endure	_____	alert	_____
affect	_____	reproduce	_____
reproduce	_____	dare	_____
crawl	_____	average	_____

외우는 게 지루하면 바로 다음 페이지로 넘어가세요!

pale [peil]	연한, 엷은
sum [sʌm]	합계
compel [kəmpél]	매력적인, 강요하다
geography [dʒiágrəfi]	지리한, 지형
flash [flæʃ]	불빛, 섬광
correspond [kɔ̀ːrəspánd]	해당하다, 일치하다
primary [práimeri]	주요한, 기본적인
fade [feid]	사라지다, 흐려지다
recommend [rèkəménd]	권고하다, 추천하다
aggressive [əgrésiv]	공격적인, 적극적인

뜻이 바로 떠오르지 않으면 왼쪽 페이지의 뜻을 보고 적으세요.

pale		sum	
flash		compel	
correspond		aggressive	
sum		primary	
primary		recommend	
fade		pale	
aggressive		aggressive	
geography		primary	
compel		recommend	
recommend		flash	
pale		correspond	
correspond		geography	
primary		sum	
compel		compel	
geography		fade	
flash		pale	
sum		aggressive	
recommend		primary	
fade		recommend	
aggressive		flash	
pale		correspond	
fade		geography	
flash		sum	
primary		compel	
recommend		fade	
aggressive		pale	
compel		flash	
correspond		correspond	
sum		sum	
geography		primary	
pale		fade	
fade		aggressive	
correspond		geography	
geography		compel	
flash		recommend	

외우는 게 지루하면 바로 다음 페이지로 넘어가세요!

vigor [vígər]	활력, 활기
critical [krítikəl]	비판적인, 중요한
analyze [aénəlàiz]	분석하다, 조사하다
riot [ráiət]	폭동, 소요
boast [boust]	자랑하다, 뽐내다
heritage [héritidʒ]	유산, 혈통
reject [ridʒékt]	거부하다, 거절하다
leak [liːk]	유출, 새다
attitude [aétitjùːd]	태도, 자세
literal [lítərəl]	글자 그대로의

뜻이 바로 떠오르지 않으면 왼쪽 페이지의 뜻을 보고 적으세요.

vigor		critical	
boast		analyze	
heritage		literal	
critical		reject	
reject		attitude	
leak		vigor	
literal		literal	
riot		reject	
analyze		attitude	
attitude		boast	
vigor		heritage	
heritage		riot	
reject		critical	
analyze		analyze	
riot		leak	
boast		vigor	
critical		literal	
attitude		reject	
leak		attitude	
literal		boast	
vigor		heritage	
leak		riot	
boast		critical	
reject		analyze	
attitude		leak	
literal		vigor	
analyze		boast	
heritage		heritage	
critical		critical	
riot		reject	
vigor		leak	
leak		literal	
heritage		riot	
riot		analyze	
boast		attitude	

외우는 게 지루하면 바로 다음 페이지로 넘어가세요!

communicate [kəmjú:nəkèit]	의사소통하다, 대화하다
duplicate [djú:plikət]	중복되다, 복제한
intrude [intrú:d]	침범하다, 방해하다
remarkable [rimá:rkəbl]	놀라운, 주목할 만한
negative [négətiv]	부정의, 음성의
rescue [réskju:]	구조하다, 구하다
budget [bʌdʒit]	예산안, 예산
fancy [faénsi]	화려한, 근사한
guilty [gílti]	유죄의, 죄책감
venture [véntʃər]	모험, 투기적 사업

뜻이 바로 떠오르지 않으면 왼쪽 페이지의 뜻을 보고 적으세요.

communicate	duplicate
negative	intrude
rescue	venture
duplicate	budget
budget	guilty
fancy	communicate
venture	venture
remarkable	budget
intrude	guilty
guilty	negative
communicate	rescue
rescue	remarkable
budget	duplicate
intrude	intrude
remarkable	fancy
negative	communicate
duplicate	venture
guilty	budget
fancy	guilty
venture	negative
communicate	rescue
fancy	remarkable
negative	duplicate
budget	intrude
guilty	fancy
venture	communicate
intrude	negative
rescue	rescue
duplicate	duplicate
remarkable	budget
communicate	fancy
fancy	venture
rescue	remarkable
remarkable	intrude
negative	guilty

trigger [trígər]	촉발, 유발하다
threat [θret]	위협, 우려
oppress [əprés]	억압하다, 탄압하다
superficial [sù:pərfíʃəl]	피상적인
prompt [prampt]	촉발하다, 신속한
valid [vǽlid]	유효한, 타당한
faint [feint]	희미한
objective [əbdʒéktiv]	목표의, 객관적인
imprison [imprízn]	가두다, 수감하다
disguise [disgáiz]	위장, 변장, 가장하다

뜻이 바로 떠오르지 않으면 왼쪽 페이지의 뜻을 보고 적으세요.

trigger		threat	
prompt		oppress	
valid		disguise	
threat		faint	
faint		imprison	
objective		trigger	
disguise		disguise	
superficial		faint	
oppress		imprison	
imprison		prompt	
trigger		valid	
valid		superficial	
faint		threat	
oppress		oppress	
superficial		objective	
prompt		trigger	
threat		disguise	
imprison		faint	
objective		imprison	
disguise		prompt	
trigger		valid	
objective		superficial	
prompt		threat	
faint		oppress	
imprison		objective	
disguise		trigger	
oppress		prompt	
valid		valid	
threat		threat	
superficial		faint	
trigger		objective	
objective		disguise	
valid		superficial	
superficial		oppress	
prompt		imprison	

외우는 게 지루하면 바로 다음 페이지로 넘어가세요!

indifferent [indífərənt]	무관심한, 무심한
apology [əpálədʒi]	사과, 사죄
stretch [stretʃ]	늘리다, 뻗다
recall [rikɔ́:l]	상기하다, 기억하다
react [riaékt]	반응하다, 대응하다
individual [ìndəvídʒuəl]	개인의, 개별의
sermon [sə́:rmən]	설교, 설법
insurance [inʃúərəns]	보험, 보험금
current [kə́:rənt]	현재의, 지금의
subscribe [səbskráib]	가입하다, 구독하다

뜻이 바로 떠오르지 않으면 왼쪽 페이지의 뜻을 보고 적으세요.

indifferent		apology	
react		stretch	
individual		subscribe	
apology		sermon	
sermon		current	
insurance		indifferent	
subscribe		subscribe	
recall		sermon	
stretch		current	
current		react	
indifferent		individual	
individual		recall	
sermon		apology	
stretch		stretch	
recall		insurance	
react		indifferent	
apology		subscribe	
current		sermon	
insurance		current	
subscribe		react	
indifferent		individual	
insurance		recall	
react		apology	
sermon		stretch	
current		insurance	
subscribe		indifferent	
stretch		react	
individual		individual	
apology		apology	
recall		sermon	
indifferent		insurance	
insurance		subscribe	
individual		recall	
recall		stretch	
react		current	

189

외우는 게 지루하면 바로 다음 페이지로 넘어가세요!

alternative [ɔ:ltə́:rnətiv]	대안, 대신의
polite [pəláit]	예의 바른, 공손한
vision [víʒən]	시야, 시력
ease [i:z]	완화하다
expand [ikspaénd]	확대하다, 확장하다
appreciate [əprí:ʃièit]	알아주다, 감사하다
candidate [kaéndidèit, -dət]	후보자, 지원자
persuade [pərswéid]	설득하다
debate [dibéit]	토론, 논쟁
property [prápərti]	특성, 재산

뜻이 바로 떠오르지 않으면 왼쪽 페이지의 뜻을 보고 적으세요.

alternative		debate	
vision		property	
expand		alternative	
persuade		expand	
property		persuade	
polite		polite	
ease		ease	
appreciate		vision	
candidate		property	
debate		debate	
property		candidate	
alternative		appreciate	
expand		alternative	
persuade		vision	
polite		expand	
ease		persuade	
vision		property	
property		ease	
debate		vision	
candidate		expand	
appreciate		polite	
alternative		persuade	
ease		debate	
vision		property	
expand		alternative	
polite		ease	
persuade		candidate	
debate		vision	
property		appreciate	
alternative		persuade	
ease		polite	
candidate		property	
vision		debate	
appreciate		expand	
persuade		appreciate	

외우는 게 지루하면 바로 다음 페이지로 넘어가세요!

float [flout]	떠오르다, 떠다니다
pressure [préʃər]	압력, 압박
excel [iksél]	뛰어나다, 두드러지다
congratulate [kəngraétʃulèit]	축하하다
automobile [ɔ̀:təməbí:l]	자동차, 차
consume [kənsú:m]	소비하다, 먹어 치우다
bias [báiəs]	편견, 치우침
rage [reidʒ]	분노
instinct [ínstiŋkt]	본능, 직감
raise [reiz]	높이다, 올리다

뜻이 바로 떠오르지 않으면 왼쪽 페이지의 뜻을 보고 적으세요.

float		pressure	
automobile		excel	
consume		raise	
pressure		bias	
bias		instinct	
rage		float	
raise		raise	
congratulate		bias	
excel		instinct	
instinct		automobile	
float		consume	
consume		congratulate	
bias		pressure	
excel		excel	
congratulate		rage	
automobile		float	
pressure		raise	
instinct		bias	
rage		instinct	
raise		automobile	
float		consume	
rage		congratulate	
automobile		pressure	
bias		excel	
instinct		rage	
raise		float	
excel		automobile	
consume		consume	
pressure		pressure	
congratulate		bias	
float		rage	
rage		raise	
consume		congratulate	
congratulate		excel	
automobile		instinct	

85

외우는 게 지루하면 바로 다음 페이지로 넘어가세요!

aside [əsáid]	이외에도, 제쳐 두고
prevail [privéil]	만연하다, 팽배하다
remove [rimúːv]	제거하다, 없애다
opportunity [ápərtjúːnəti]	기회, 찬스
minor [máinər]	소수의, 사소한
encounter [inkáuntər]	만나다, 마주치다
confine [kənfáin]	국한하다, 제한하다
isolate [áisəlèit]	분리하다, 고립시키다
caution [kɔ́ːʃən]	주의, 경고
stare [stɛər]	쳐다보다, 바라보다

194

뜻이 바로 떠오르지 않으면 왼쪽 페이지의 뜻을 보고 적으세요.

aside		prevail	
minor		remove	
encounter		stare	
prevail		confine	
confine		caution	
isolate		aside	
stare		stare	
opportunity		confine	
remove		caution	
caution		minor	
aside		encounter	
encounter		opportunity	
confine		prevail	
remove		remove	
opportunity		isolate	
minor		aside	
prevail		stare	
caution		confine	
isolate		caution	
stare		minor	
aside		encounter	
isolate		opportunity	
minor		prevail	
confine		remove	
caution		isolate	
stare		aside	
remove		minor	
encounter		encounter	
prevail		prevail	
opportunity		confine	
aside		isolate	
isolate		stare	
encounter		opportunity	
opportunity		remove	
minor		caution	

외우는 게 지루하면 바로 다음 페이지로 넘어가세요!

crisis [kráisis]	위기, 문제
immediate [imí:diət]	즉각적인, 즉시
relative [rélətiv]	상대적인, 관련된
diagnose [dáiəgnòus]	진단하다, 규명하다
illusion [ilú:ʒən]	착각, 환상
divine [diváin]	신의, 신성한
polish [páliʃ]	닦다, 세련되게 하다
scold [skould]	꾸짖다, 혼내다
prey [prei]	먹이, 사냥
compete [kəmpí:t]	경쟁하다, 경기하다

뜻이 바로 떠오르지 않으면 왼쪽 페이지의 뜻을 보고 적으세요.

crisis		immediate	
illusion		relative	
divine		compete	
immediate		polish	
polish		prey	
scold		crisis	
compete		compete	
diagnose		polish	
relative		prey	
prey		illusion	
crisis		divine	
divine		diagnose	
polish		immediate	
relative		relative	
diagnose		scold	
illusion		crisis	
immediate		compete	
prey		polish	
scold		prey	
compete		illusion	
crisis		divine	
scold		diagnose	
illusion		immediate	
polish		relative	
prey		scold	
compete		crisis	
relative		illusion	
divine		divine	
immediate		immediate	
diagnose		polish	
crisis		scold	
scold		compete	
divine		diagnose	
diagnose		relative	
illusion		prey	

외우는 게 지루하면 바로 다음 페이지로 넘어가세요!

surface [sə́:rfis]	표면, 지표의
domestic [dəméstik]	국내의, 가정의
engage [ingéidʒ]	관여하다, 약혼하다
relax [rilaéks]	편안해지다, 쉬다
positive [pázətiv]	긍정적인, 확신 있는
era [íərə, érə]	시대, 시절
overall [ouˈvərəˌl]	전반적으로
due [djuː]	예정인, 정당한
awake [əwéik]	깨다, 잠에서 깨다
abstract [æbstraékt]	추상적인

뜻이 바로 떠오르지 않으면 왼쪽 페이지의 뜻을 보고 적으세요.

surface		domestic	
positive		engage	
era		abstract	
domestic		overall	
overall		awake	
due		surface	
abstract		abstract	
relax		overall	
engage		awake	
awake		positive	
surface		era	
era		relax	
overall		domestic	
engage		engage	
relax		due	
positive		surface	
domestic		abstract	
awake		overall	
due		awake	
abstract		positive	
surface		era	
due		relax	
positive		domestic	
overall		engage	
awake		due	
abstract		surface	
engage		positive	
era		era	
domestic		domestic	
relax		overall	
surface		due	
due		abstract	
era		relax	
relax		engage	
positive		awake	

외우는 게 지루하면 바로 다음 페이지로 넘어가세요!

exotic [igzátik]	이국적인
undertake [əˈndərteiˌk]	착수하다, 떠맡다
refund [rifʌnd]	환불하다, 환급하다
compliment [kámpləmənt]	칭찬하다, 찬사
torture [tɔ́ːrtʃər]	고문, 고통을 주다
trait [treit]	특징, 특성
still [stil]	여전히, 아직도
reverse [rivə́ːrs]	반대의, 뒤집다
manufacture [mænjufaɛ́ktʃər]	생산, 산업
suspect [səspékt]	의심하다, 용의자

뜻이 바로 떠오르지 않으면 왼쪽 페이지의 뜻을 보고 적으세요.

exotic		undertake	
torture		refund	
trait		suspect	
undertake		still	
still		manufacture	
reverse		exotic	
suspect		suspect	
compliment		still	
refund		manufacture	
manufacture		torture	
exotic		trait	
trait		compliment	
still		undertake	
refund		refund	
compliment		reverse	
torture		exotic	
undertake		suspect	
manufacture		still	
reverse		manufacture	
suspect		torture	
exotic		trait	
reverse		compliment	
torture		undertake	
still		refund	
manufacture		reverse	
suspect		exotic	
refund		torture	
trait		trait	
undertake		undertake	
compliment		still	
exotic		reverse	
reverse		suspect	
trait		compliment	
compliment		refund	
torture		manufacture	

외우는 게 지루하면 바로 다음 페이지로 넘어가세요!

fit [fit]	꼭 맞는, 부합
author [ɔ́ːθər]	작가, 저자
adjust [ədʒʌ́st]	조정되다, 적응하다
sacrifice [saékrəfàis]	희생, 제물
postpone [poustpóun]	연기하다, 미루다
frequent [fríːkwənt]	자주, 잦은
humble [hʌ́mbl]	겸손한, 초라한
suck [sʌk]	빨다, 형편없다
protect [prətékt]	보호하다, 지키다
justice [dʒʌ́stis]	정의, 사법

뜻이 바로 떠오르지 않으면 왼쪽 페이지의 뜻을 보고 적으세요.

fit		author	
postpone		adjust	
frequent		justice	
author		humble	
humble		protect	
suck		fit	
justice		justice	
sacrifice		humble	
adjust		protect	
protect		postpone	
fit		frequent	
frequent		sacrifice	
humble		author	
adjust		adjust	
sacrifice		suck	
postpone		fit	
author		justice	
protect		humble	
suck		protect	
justice		postpone	
fit		frequent	
suck		sacrifice	
postpone		author	
humble		adjust	
protect		suck	
justice		fit	
adjust		postpone	
frequent		frequent	
author		author	
sacrifice		humble	
fit		suck	
suck		justice	
frequent		sacrifice	
sacrifice		adjust	
postpone		protect	

외우는 게 지루하면 바로 다음 페이지로 넘어가세요!

upright [ʌ́pràit]	똑바로, 직립한
formal [fɔ́ːrməl]	공식적인, 정식의
cure [kjuər]	치료, 양생
insect [ínsekt]	곤충, 벌레
rub [rʌb]	문지르다, 바르다
overlook [ouˈvərluˌk]	간과하다, 눈감아 주다
advocate [aédvəkèit]	옹호하다, 주장하다
swell [swel]	붓다, 붓기
strain [strein]	압력, 압박
prime [praim]	주요한

뜻이 바로 떠오르지 않으면 왼쪽 페이지의 뜻을 보고 적으세요.

upright	formal	
rub	cure	
overlook	prime	
formal	advocate	
advocate	strain	
swell	upright	
prime	prime	
insect	advocate	
cure	strain	
strain	rub	
upright	overlook	
overlook	insect	
advocate	formal	
cure	cure	
insect	swell	
rub	upright	
formal	prime	
strain	advocate	
swell	strain	
prime	rub	
upright	overlook	
swell	insect	
rub	formal	
advocate	cure	
strain	swell	
prime	upright	
cure	rub	
overlook	overlook	
formal	formal	
insect	advocate	
upright	swell	
swell	prime	
overlook	insect	
insect	cure	
rub	strain	

외우는 게 지루하면 바로 다음 페이지로 넘어가세요!

mode [moud]	형태, 방법
unify [júːnəfài]	통일하다, 통합하다
typical [típikəl]	전형적인, 일반적인
obey [oubéi]	따르다, 준수하다
trap [træp]	가두다, 덫
fluid [flúːid]	유동성의
sustain [səstéin]	지속하다, 지탱하다
shift [ʃift]	변화, 전환
alter [ɔ́ːltər]	바꾸다, 변경하다
drown [draun]	익사하다, 물에 빠지다

뜻이 바로 떠오르지 않으면 왼쪽 페이지의 뜻을 보고 적으세요.

mode	unify	
trap	typical	
fluid	drown	
unify	sustain	
sustain	alter	
shift	mode	
drown	drown	
obey	sustain	
typical	alter	
alter	trap	
mode	fluid	
fluid	obey	
sustain	unify	
typical	typical	
obey	shift	
trap	mode	
unify	drown	
alter	sustain	
shift	alter	
drown	trap	
mode	fluid	
shift	obey	
trap	unify	
sustain	typical	
alter	shift	
drown	mode	
typical	trap	
fluid	fluid	
unify	unify	
obey	sustain	
mode	shift	
shift	drown	
fluid	obey	
obey	typical	
trap	alter	

외우는 게 지루하면 바로 다음 페이지로 넘어가세요!

intimate [íntəmət]	친밀한, 사적인
require [rikwáiər]	필요하다, 요구하다
ridiculous [ridíkjuləs]	터무니없는
subject [sʌ́bdʒikt]	과목, 주제
economy [ikánəmi]	경제, 경기
outlet [áutlet, -lit]	배출구, 출구
compassion [kəmpaéʃən]	동정, 연민
consist [kənsíst]	이루어지다, 구성되다
adolescent [ædəlésnt]	청소년, 청년
client [kláiənt]	고객, 클라이언트

뜻이 바로 떠오르지 않으면 왼쪽 페이지의 뜻을 보고 적으세요.

intimate		require	
economy		ridiculous	
outlet		client	
require		compassion	
compassion		adolescent	
consist		intimate	
client		client	
subject		compassion	
ridiculous		adolescent	
adolescent		economy	
intimate		outlet	
outlet		subject	
compassion		require	
ridiculous		ridiculous	
subject		consist	
economy		intimate	
require		client	
adolescent		compassion	
consist		adolescent	
client		economy	
intimate		outlet	
consist		subject	
economy		require	
compassion		ridiculous	
adolescent		consist	
client		intimate	
ridiculous		economy	
outlet		outlet	
require		require	
subject		compassion	
intimate		consist	
consist		client	
outlet		subject	
subject		ridiculous	
economy		adolescent	

외우는 게 지루하면 바로 다음 페이지로 넘어가세요!

research [risə́:rtʃ]	연구, 조사
consider [kənsídər]	고려하다
attempt [ətémpt]	시도하다, 노력
feature [fí:tʃər]	특징, 출연하다
enhance [inhaéns]	향상하다, 강화하다
stand [stænd]	세우다, 서다
biology [baiálədʒi]	생물학
draw [drɔ:]	그리다, 끌다
reward [riwɔ́:rd]	보상, 대가
logic [ládʒik]	논리, 생각

뜻이 바로 떠오르지 않으면 왼쪽 페이지의 뜻을 보고 적으세요.

research		consider	
enhance		attempt	
stand		logic	
consider		biology	
biology		reward	
draw		research	
logic		logic	
feature		biology	
attempt		reward	
reward		enhance	
research		stand	
stand		feature	
biology		consider	
attempt		attempt	
feature		draw	
enhance		research	
consider		logic	
reward		biology	
draw		reward	
logic		enhance	
research		stand	
draw		feature	
enhance		consider	
biology		attempt	
reward		draw	
logic		research	
attempt		enhance	
stand		stand	
consider		consider	
feature		biology	
research		draw	
draw		logic	
stand		feature	
feature		attempt	
enhance		reward	

외우는 게 지루하면 바로 다음 페이지로 넘어가세요!

sacred [séikrid]	신성한, 성스러운
vain [vein]	헛된
block [blak]	차단, 막다
present [préznt]	현재의, 보여 주다
telescope [téləskòup]	망원경, 현미경
nutrition [njuːtríʃən]	영양, 식생활
perspective [pərspéktiv]	관점, 시각
betray [bitréi]	배신하다, 배반하다
narrow [naérou]	좁은, 줄이다
pour [pɔːr]	붓다, 따르다

뜻이 바로 떠오르지 않으면 왼쪽 페이지의 뜻을 보고 적으세요.

sacred		vain	
telescope		block	
nutrition		pour	
vain		perspective	
perspective		narrow	
betray		sacred	
pour		pour	
present		perspective	
block		narrow	
narrow		telescope	
sacred		nutrition	
nutrition		present	
perspective		vain	
block		block	
present		betray	
telescope		sacred	
vain		pour	
narrow		perspective	
betray		narrow	
pour		telescope	
sacred		nutrition	
betray		present	
telescope		vain	
perspective		block	
narrow		betray	
pour		sacred	
block		telescope	
nutrition		nutrition	
vain		vain	
present		perspective	
sacred		betray	
betray		pour	
nutrition		present	
present		block	
telescope		narrow	

외우는 게 지루하면 바로 다음 페이지로 넘어가세요!

border [bɔ́ːrdər]	국경, 경계
evil [íːvəl]	사악한, 악마
innocent [ínəsənt]	죄 없는, 순수한
spread [spred]	퍼지다, 확산되다
inevitable [inévətəbl]	불가피한, 피할 수 없는
trial [tráiəl]	실험, 시험
landscape [lǽndsk,eɪpə]	경관, 풍경
chase [tʃeis]	쫓다, 쫓아내다
reflect [riflékt]	반영하다, 보여 주다
supply [səplái]	공급하다, 물품

뜻이 바로 떠오르지 않으면 왼쪽 페이지의 뜻을 보고 적으세요.

border		evil	
inevitable		innocent	
trial		supply	
evil		landscape	
landscape		reflect	
chase		border	
supply		supply	
spread		landscape	
innocent		reflect	
reflect		inevitable	
border		trial	
trial		spread	
landscape		evil	
innocent		innocent	
spread		chase	
inevitable		border	
evil		supply	
reflect		landscape	
chase		reflect	
supply		inevitable	
border		trial	
chase		spread	
inevitable		evil	
landscape		innocent	
reflect		chase	
supply		border	
innocent		inevitable	
trial		trial	
evil		evil	
spread		landscape	
border		chase	
chase		supply	
trial		spread	
spread		innocent	
inevitable		reflect	

외우는 게 지루하면 바로 다음 페이지로 넘어가세요!

constitute [kánstətjùːt]	구성하다, 간주하다
altitude [aéltətjùːd]	고도, 고지
measure [méʒər]	측정하다, 대책
defeat [difíːt]	패배시키다
claim [kleim]	주장하다, 요구하다
radical [raédikəl]	급진적인, 과격한
shrink [ʃriŋk]	줄다, 감소하다
compromise [kámprəmàiz]	타협하다, 절충하다
flame [fleim]	화염, 불꽃
ingredient [ingríːdiənt]	재료, 성분

뜻이 바로 떠오르지 않으면 왼쪽 페이지의 뜻을 보고 적으세요.

constitute	altitude
claim	measure
radical	ingredient
altitude	shrink
shrink	flame
compromise	constitute
ingredient	ingredient
defeat	shrink
measure	flame
flame	claim
constitute	radical
radical	defeat
shrink	altitude
measure	measure
defeat	compromise
claim	constitute
altitude	ingredient
flame	shrink
compromise	flame
ingredient	claim
constitute	radical
compromise	defeat
claim	altitude
shrink	measure
flame	compromise
ingredient	constitute
measure	claim
radical	radical
altitude	altitude
defeat	shrink
constitute	compromise
compromise	ingredient
radical	defeat
defeat	measure
claim	flame

외우는 게 지루하면 바로 다음 페이지로 넘어가세요!

attend [əténd]	참석하다
oppose [əpóuz]	반대하다, 대항하다
lean [li:n]	기울어지다, 기대다
dimension [diménʃən]	차원, 부피
influence [ínfluəns]	영향, 요인
esteem [istí:m]	존중하다, 평가하다
gratitude [graétətjù:d]	감사, 고마움
companion [kəmpaénjən]	동반자, 친구
function [fʌ́ŋkʃən]	기능, 역할
refer [rifə́:r]	말하다, 언급하다

뜻이 바로 떠오르지 않으면 왼쪽 페이지의 뜻을 보고 적으세요.

attend		oppose	
influence		lean	
esteem		refer	
oppose		gratitude	
gratitude		function	
companion		attend	
refer		refer	
dimension		gratitude	
lean		function	
function		influence	
attend		esteem	
esteem		dimension	
gratitude		oppose	
lean		lean	
dimension		companion	
influence		attend	
oppose		refer	
function		gratitude	
companion		function	
refer		influence	
attend		esteem	
companion		dimension	
influence		oppose	
gratitude		lean	
function		companion	
refer		attend	
lean		influence	
esteem		esteem	
oppose		oppose	
dimension		gratitude	
attend		companion	
companion		refer	
esteem		dimension	
dimension		lean	
influence		function	

외우는 게 지루하면 바로 다음 페이지로 넘어가세요!

origin [ɔ́:rədʒin]	기원
classify [klǽsəfài]	분류하다
imitate [ímətèit]	모방하다, 흉내 내다
commodity [kəmádəti]	상품, 원자재
peer [piər]	동료
consent [kənsént]	동의하다, 승낙하다
gather [gǽðər]	수집하다, 모이다
hatch [hætʃ]	부화하다
protest [próutest]	시위, 항의
restore [ristɔ́:r]	복원하다, 회복하다

뜻이 바로 떠오르지 않으면 왼쪽 페이지의 뜻을 보고 적으세요.

origin		classify	
peer		imitate	
consent		restore	
classify		gather	
gather		protest	
hatch		origin	
restore		restore	
commodity		gather	
imitate		protest	
protest		peer	
origin		consent	
consent		commodity	
gather		classify	
imitate		imitate	
commodity		hatch	
peer		origin	
classify		restore	
protest		gather	
hatch		protest	
restore		peer	
origin		consent	
hatch		commodity	
peer		classify	
gather		imitate	
protest		hatch	
restore		origin	
imitate		peer	
consent		consent	
classify		classity	
commodity		gather	
origin		hatch	
hatch		restore	
consent		commodity	
commodity		imitate	
peer		protest	

외우는 게 지루하면 바로 다음 페이지로 넘어가세요!

manipulate [mənípjulèit]	조작하다, 조종하다
numerous [ˊnuːmərəs]	수많은, 다양한
entire [intáiər]	전체의
verbal [vɜ́ːrbəl]	말의, 진술의
glitter [glítər]	반짝이다, 화려하다
prove [pruːv]	증명하다, 입증하다
enormous [inɔ́ːrməs]	엄청난, 거대한
forecast [fɔ'rkæˌst]	예상, 전망하다
spirit [spírit]	정신
superstition [sùːpərstíʃən]	미신

뜻이 바로 떠오르지 않으면 왼쪽 페이지의 뜻을 보고 적으세요.

manipulate		numerous	
glitter		entire	
prove		superstition	
numerous		enormous	
enormous		spirit	
forecast		manipulate	
superstition		superstition	
verbal		enormous	
entire		spirit	
spirit		glitter	
manipulate		prove	
prove		verbal	
enormous		numerous	
entire		entire	
verbal		forecast	
glitter		manipulate	
numerous		superstition	
spirit		enormous	
forecast		spirit	
superstition		glitter	
manipulate		prove	
forecast		verbal	
glitter		numerous	
enormous		entire	
spirit		forecast	
superstition		manipulate	
entire		glitter	
prove		prove	
numerous		numerous	
verbal		enormous	
manipulate		forecast	
forecast		superstition	
prove		verbal	
verbal		entire	
glitter		spirit	

외우는 게 지루하면 바로 다음 페이지로 넘어가세요!

negotiate [nigóuʃièit]	협상하다, 협의하다
contrast [kəntraést]	대조, 대비
empire [émpaiər]	제국, 왕국
overcome [ouˈvərkəˌm]	극복하다, 이겨 내다
infant [ínfənt]	유아의, 초기 단계의
prosper [práspər]	번영하다, 발전하다
magnificent [mægnífəsnt]	멋진, 아름다운
method [méθəd]	방법, 방식
pierce [piərs]	뚫다, 꽂다
translate [trænsléit]	번역하다, 옮기다

뜻이 바로 떠오르지 않으면 왼쪽 페이지의 뜻을 보고 적으세요.

negotiate		contrast	
infant		empire	
prosper		translate	
contrast		magnificent	
magnificent		pierce	
method		negotiate	
translate		translate	
overcome		magnificent	
empire		pierce	
pierce		infant	
negotiate		prosper	
prosper		overcome	
magnificent		contrast	
empire		empire	
overcome		method	
infant		negotiate	
contrast		translate	
pierce		magnificent	
method		pierce	
translate		infant	
negotiate		prosper	
method		overcome	
infant		contrast	
magnificent		empire	
pierce		method	
translate		negotiate	
empire		infant	
prosper		prosper	
contrast		contrast	
overcome		magnificent	
negotiate		method	
method		translate	
prosper		overcome	
overcome		empire	
infant		pierce	

외우는 게 지루하면 바로 다음 페이지로 넘어가세요!

heredity [hərédəti]	유전, 세습	
duty [djúːti]	의무, 임무	
desperate [déspərət]	필사적인, 절실한	
tact [tækt]	재치, 재주	
factor [faéktər]	요인, 원인	
element [éləmənt]	요소, 원소	
prospect [práspekt]	전망, 과제	
divorce [divɔ́ːrs]	이혼, 분리	
prominent [prámənənt]	유명한, 두드러진	
operate [ápərèit]	운영하다, 영업하다	

뜻이 바로 떠오르지 않으면 왼쪽 페이지의 뜻을 보고 적으세요.

heredity		duty	
factor		desperate	
element		operate	
duty		prospect	
prospect		prominent	
divorce		heredity	
operate		operate	
tact		prospect	
desperate		prominent	
prominent		factor	
heredity		element	
element		tact	
prospect		duty	
desperate		desperate	
tact		divorce	
factor		heredity	
duty		operate	
prominent		prospect	
divorce		prominent	
operate		factor	
heredity		element	
divorce		tact	
factor		duty	
prospect		desperate	
prominent		divorce	
operate		heredity	
desperate		factor	
element		element	
duty		duty	
tact		prospect	
heredity		divorce	
divorce		operate	
element		tact	
tact		desperate	
factor		prominent	

외우는 게 지루하면 바로 다음 페이지로 넘어가세요!

particle [páːrtikl]	입자, 먼지
accuse [əkjúːz]	비난하다, 고소하다
observe [əbzə́ːrv]	관찰하다, 보다
germ [dʒəːrm]	세균, 병균
utmost [ʌ́tmòust]	최선, 최대한
colony [káləni]	식민지
explode [iksplóud]	폭발하다, 터지다
aspire [əspáiər]	열망하다, 갈망하다
substitute [sʌ́bstətjùːt]	대체하다, 대신
stable [stéibl]	안정적인

뜻이 바로 떠오르지 않으면 왼쪽 페이지의 뜻을 보고 적으세요.

particle		accuse	
utmost		observe	
colony		stable	
accuse		explode	
explode		substitute	
aspire		particle	
stable		stable	
germ		explode	
observe		substitute	
substitute		utmost	
particle		colony	
colony		germ	
explode		accuse	
observe		observe	
germ		aspire	
utmost		particle	
accuse		stable	
substitute		explode	
aspire		substitute	
stable		utmost	
particle		colony	
aspire		germ	
utmost		accuse	
explode		observe	
substitute		aspire	
stable		particle	
observe		utmost	
colony		colony	
accuse		accuse	
germ		explode	
particle		aspire	
aspire		stable	
colony		germ	
germ		observe	
utmost		substitute	

외우는 게 지루하면 바로 다음 페이지로 넘어가세요!

obvious [ábviəs]	분명한, 명백한
improve [imprúːv]	개선하다, 향상하다
cottage [kátidʒ]	집의, 오두막
blossom [blásəm]	꽃, 피다
ultimate [ʌltəmət]	궁극적인, 최종의
haunt [hɔːnt]	괴롭히다
provide [prəváid]	제공하다, 공급하다
defect [díːfekt]	결함, 장애
comment [káment]	말, 발언
presume [prizúːm]	추정하다, 가정하다

뜻이 바로 떠오르지 않으면 왼쪽 페이지의 뜻을 보고 적으세요.

obvious		improve	
ultimate		cottage	
haunt		presume	
improve		provide	
provide		comment	
defect		obvious	
presume		presume	
blossom		provide	
cottage		comment	
comment		ultimate	
obvious		haunt	
haunt		blossom	
provide		improve	
cottage		cottage	
blossom		defect	
ultimate		obvious	
improve		presume	
comment		provide	
defect		comment	
presume		ultimate	
obvious		haunt	
defect		blossom	
ultimate		improve	
provide		cottage	
comment		defect	
presume		obvious	
cottage		ultimate	
haunt		haunt	
improve		improve	
blossom		provide	
obvious		defect	
defect		presume	
haunt		blossom	
blossom		cottage	
ultimate		comment	

외우는 게 지루하면 바로 다음 페이지로 넘어가세요!

select [silékt]	선택하다, 선발하다
visual [víʒuəl]	시각의, 눈에 보이는
laboratory [laébərətɔ̀:ri]	연구실, 실험실
major [méidʒər]	주요한, 큰
scream [skri:m]	비명, 절규
species [spí:ʃi:z]	종, 종류
bless [bles]	축복하다, 감사하다
despite [dispáit]	불구하고
despair [dispéər]	절망, 좌절
describe [diskráib]	묘사하다, 설명하다

뜻이 바로 떠오르지 않으면 왼쪽 페이지의 뜻을 보고 적으세요.

select		visual	
scream		laboratory	
species		describe	
visual		bless	
bless		despair	
despite		select	
describe		describe	
major		bless	
laboratory		despair	
despair		scream	
select		species	
species		major	
bless		visual	
laboratory		laboratory	
major		despite	
scream		select	
visual		describe	
despair		bless	
despite		despair	
describe		scream	
select		species	
despite		major	
scream		visual	
bless		laboratory	
despair		despite	
describe		select	
laboratory		scream	
species		species	
visual		visual	
major		bless	
select		despite	
despite		describe	
species		major	
major		laboratory	
scream		despair	

외우는 게 지루하면 바로 다음 페이지로 넘어가세요!

utter [ʌtər]	말하다, 완전한
deceive [disíːv]	속이다, 기만하다
calculate [kaélkjulèit]	계산하다, 산정하다
promote [prəmóut]	홍보하다, 촉진하다
carve [kaːrv]	조각하다, 자르다
contain [kəntéin]	들어 있다, 포함하다
discriminate [diskrímənèit]	차별하다, 식별하다
instrument [ínstrəmənt]	악기, 도구
persist [pərsíst]	고집하다, 지속하다
compulsory [kəmpʌ́lsəri]	의무적인, 강제적인

뜻이 바로 떠오르지 않으면 왼쪽 페이지의 뜻을 보고 적으세요.

utter		deceive	
carve		calculate	
contain		compulsory	
deceive		discriminate	
discriminate		persist	
instrument		utter	
compulsory		compulsory	
promote		discriminate	
calculate		persist	
persist		carve	
utter		contain	
contain		promote	
discriminate		deceive	
calculate		calculate	
promote		instrument	
carve		utter	
deceive		compulsory	
persist		discriminate	
instrument		persist	
compulsory		carve	
utter		contain	
instrument		promote	
carve		deceive	
discriminate		calculate	
persist		instrument	
compulsory		utter	
calculate		carve	
contain		contain	
deceive		deceive	
promote		discriminate	
utter		instrument	
instrument		compulsory	
contain		promote	
promote		calculate	
carve		persist	

외우는 게 지루하면 바로 다음 페이지로 넘어가세요!

leap [liːp]	도약하다, 건너뛰다
reluctant [rilʌ́ktənt]	꺼리는, 주저하는
conduct [kándʌkt]	실시하다, 수행하다
ancestor [aénsestər]	조상, 선조
flexible [fléksəbl]	유연한, 신축성 있는
riddle [rídl]	수수께끼
exceed [iksíːd]	넘어서다, 초과하다
reveal [rivíːl]	보여 주다, 드러내다
bear [bɛər]	참다, 견디다
transport [trænspɔ́ːrt]	운송하다, 교통

leap		reluctant	
flexible		conduct	
riddle		transport	
reluctant		exceed	
exceed		bear	
reveal		leap	
transport		transport	
ancestor		exceed	
conduct		bear	
bear		flexible	
leap		riddle	
riddle		ancestor	
exceed		reluctant	
conduct		conduct	
ancestor		reveal	
flexible		leap	
reluctant		transport	
bear		exceed	
reveal		bear	
transport		flexible	
leap		riddle	
reveal		ancestor	
flexible		reluctant	
exceed		conduct	
bear		reveal	
transport		leap	
conduct		flexible	
riddle		riddle	
reluctant		reluctant	
ancestor		exceed	
leap		reveal	
reveal		transport	
riddle		ancestor	
ancestor		conduct	
flexible		bear	

외우는 게 지루하면 바로 다음 페이지로 넘어가세요!

digest [didʒést, dai-]	소화하다
ethical [éθikəl]	윤리의, 도덕의
owe [ou]	빚지다, 신세 지다
portion [pɔ́ːrʃən]	부분, 일부
inhabit [inhaébit]	거주하다, 서식하다
honesty [ánisti]	정직, 솔직
prejudice [prédʒudis]	편견, 선입관
convert [kənvə́ːrt]	전환하다, 바꾸다
novel [návəl]	소설
accelerate [æksélərèit]	가속하다, 빨라지다

뜻이 바로 떠오르지 않으면 왼쪽 페이지의 뜻을 보고 적으세요.

digest		ethical	
inhabit		owe	
honesty		accelerate	
ethical		prejudice	
prejudice		novel	
convert		digest	
accelerate		accelerate	
portion		prejudice	
owe		novel	
novel		inhabit	
digest		honesty	
honesty		portion	
prejudice		ethical	
owe		owe	
portion		convert	
inhabit		digest	
ethical		accelerate	
novel		prejudice	
convert		novel	
accelerate		inhabit	
digest		honesty	
convert		portion	
inhabit		ethical	
prejudice		owe	
novel		convert	
accelerate		digest	
owe		inhabit	
honesty		honesty	
ethical		ethical	
portion		prejudice	
digest		convert	
convert		accelerate	
honesty		portion	
portion		owe	
inhabit		novel	

외우는 게 지루하면 바로 다음 페이지로 넘어가세요!

infinite [ínfənət]	무한한, 끝없는
erect [irékt]	세우다, 건설하다
prevent [privént]	막다, 방지하다
agenda [ədʒéndə]	의제, 과제
naked [néikid]	벌거벗은, 나체의
combine [kəmbáin]	결합시키다, 합치다
fierce [fiərs]	치열한, 거센
maintain [meintéin]	유지하다, 계속하다
obstacle [ábstəkl]	장애, 방해
exaggerate [igzaédʒərèit]	과장하다, 지나친

뜻이 바로 떠오르지 않으면 왼쪽 페이지의 뜻을 보고 적으세요.

infinite		erect	
naked		prevent	
combine		exaggerate	
erect		fierce	
fierce		obstacle	
maintain		infinite	
exaggerate		exaggerate	
agenda		fierce	
prevent		obstacle	
obstacle		naked	
infinite		combine	
combine		agenda	
fierce		erect	
prevent		prevent	
agenda		maintain	
naked		infinite	
erect		exaggerate	
obstacle		fierce	
maintain		obstacle	
exaggerate		naked	
infinite		combine	
maintain		agenda	
naked		erect	
fierce		prevent	
obstacle		maintain	
exaggerate		infinite	
prevent		naked	
combine		combine	
erect		erect	
agenda		fierce	
infinite		maintain	
maintain		exaggerate	
combine		agenda	
agenda		prevent	
naked		obstacle	

외우는 게 지루하면 바로 다음 페이지로 넘어가세요!

ancient [éinʃənt]	고대의, 오래된
dumb [dʌm]	멍청한, 말이 없는
greed [griːd]	탐욕, 욕심
heir [ɛər]	후계자
curse [kəːrs]	저주, 욕설
intent [intént]	의도, 의향
crime [kraim]	범죄, 죄
fault [fɔːlt]	고장, 잘못
prior [práiər]	전의, 앞서
identify [aidéntəfài]	확인하다, 알아보다

뜻이 바로 떠오르지 않으면 왼쪽 페이지의 뜻을 보고 적으세요.

ancient		dumb	
curse		greed	
intent		identify	
dumb		crime	
crime		prior	
fault		ancient	
identify		identify	
heir		crime	
greed		prior	
prior		curse	
ancient		intent	
intent		heir	
crime		dumb	
greed		greed	
heir		fault	
curse		ancient	
dumb		identify	
prior		crime	
fault		prior	
identify		curse	
ancient		intent	
fault		heir	
curse		dumb	
crime		greed	
prior		fault	
identify		ancient	
greed		curse	
intent		intent	
dumb		dumb	
heir		crime	
ancient		fault	
fault		identify	
intent		heir	
heir		greed	
curse		prior	

외우는 게 지루하면 바로 다음 페이지로 넘어가세요!

drought [draut]	가뭄, 고갈
sensible [sénsəbl]	현명한, 합리적인
smash [smæʃ]	부서지다, 깨다
criticism [krítəsìzm]	비판, 비난
temperature [témpərətʃər]	온도, 열
comfort [kʌmfərt]	위로, 편안함
ally [əlái]	동맹, 연합
approximate [əpráksəmət]	대강의, 가까운
submit [səbmít]	제출하다, 제시하다
stain [stein]	얼룩, 오염

뜻이 바로 떠오르지 않으면 왼쪽 페이지의 뜻을 보고 적으세요.

drought		sensible	
temperature		smash	
comfort		stain	
sensible		ally	
ally		submit	
approximate		drought	
stain		stain	
criticism		ally	
smash		submit	
submit		temperature	
drought		comfort	
comfort		criticism	
ally		sensible	
smash		smash	
criticism		approximate	
temperature		drought	
sensible		stain	
submit		ally	
approximate		submit	
stain		temperature	
drought		comfort	
approximate		criticism	
temperature		sensible	
ally		smash	
submit		approximate	
stain		drought	
smash		temperature	
comfort		comfort	
sensible		sensible	
criticism		ally	
drought		approximate	
approximate		stain	
comfort		criticism	
criticism		smash	
temperature		submit	

외우는 게 지루하면 바로 다음 페이지로 넘어가세요!

tradition [trədíʃən]	전통, 관습
overtake [ouˈvərteiˌk]	추월하다, 제치다
habitat [haébitæt]	서식지, 생태
independent [ìndipéndənt]	독립한, 무소속의
cradle [kréidl]	요람, 어린 시절
soar [sɔːr]	치솟다, 증가하다
repair [ripéər]	수리, 치료하다
compound [kámpaund]	화합물, 복합의
adequate [aédikwət]	적당한, 충분한
fertile [fɔ́ːrtl]	비옥한, 가임의

뜻이 바로 떠오르지 않으면 왼쪽 페이지의 뜻을 보고 적으세요.

tradition		overtake	
cradle		habitat	
soar		fertile	
overtake		repair	
repair		adequate	
compound		tradition	
fertile		fertile	
independent		repair	
habitat		adequate	
adequate		cradle	
tradition		soar	
soar		independent	
repair		overtake	
habitat		habitat	
independent		compound	
cradle		tradition	
overtake		fertile	
adequate		repair	
compound		adequate	
fertile		cradle	
tradition		soar	
compound		independent	
cradle		overtake	
repair		habitat	
adequate		compound	
fertile		tradition	
habitat		cradle	
soar		soar	
overtake		overtake	
independent		repair	
tradition		compound	
compound		fertile	
soar		independent	
independent		habitat	
cradle		adequate	

외우는 게 지루하면 바로 다음 페이지로 넘어가세요!

awkward [ɔ́:kwərd]	어색한, 거북한
ordinary [ɔ́:rdənèri]	일반적인, 평범한
lessen [lésn]	줄이다, 완화하다
distinct [distíŋkt]	뚜렷한, 다른
atmosphere [aétməsfìər]	대기, 분위기
restrict [ristríkt]	제한하다, 규제
liberal [líbərəl]	진보적인, 자유로운
retire [ritáiər]	은퇴하다, 퇴직하다
tribe [traib]	부족, 집단
orbit [ɔ́:rbit]	궤도

뜻이 바로 떠오르지 않으면 왼쪽 페이지의 뜻을 보고 적으세요.

awkward		ordinary	
atmosphere		lessen	
restrict		orbit	
ordinary		liberal	
liberal		tribe	
retire		awkward	
orbit		orbit	
distinct		liberal	
lessen		tribe	
tribe		atmosphere	
awkward		restrict	
restrict		distinct	
liberal		ordinary	
lessen		lessen	
distinct		retire	
atmosphere		awkward	
ordinary		orbit	
tribe		liberal	
retire		tribe	
orbit		atmosphere	
awkward		restrict	
retire		distinct	
atmosphere		ordinary	
liberal		lessen	
tribe		retire	
orbit		awkward	
lessen		atmosphere	
restrict		restrict	
ordinary		ordinary	
distinct		liberal	
awkward		retire	
retire		orbit	
restrict		distinct	
distinct		lessen	
atmosphere		tribe	

sink [siŋk]	침몰하다, 가라앉다
implement [ímpləmənt]	시행하다, 실행하다
device [diváis]	장치, 기기
glance [glæns]	흘끗 보다
specialize [spéʃəlàiz]	전문화하다
genius [dʒíːnjəs]	천재, 비범한
contribute [kəntríbjuːt]	기여하다, 공헌하다
behalf [biháéf]	이익, 원조
compare [kəmpéər]	비교하다, 비유하다
dump [dʌmp]	버리다, 쓰레기 더미

뜻이 바로 떠오르지 않으면 왼쪽 페이지의 뜻을 보고 적으세요.

sink		implement	
specialize		device	
genius		dump	
implement		contribute	
contribute		compare	
behalf		sink	
dump		dump	
glance		contribute	
device		compare	
compare		specialize	
sink		genius	
genius		glance	
contribute		implement	
device		device	
glance		behalf	
specialize		sink	
implement		dump	
compare		contribute	
behalf		compare	
dump		specialize	
sink		genius	
behalf		glance	
specialize		implement	
contribute		device	
compare		behalf	
dump		sink	
device		specialize	
genius		genius	
implement		implement	
glance		contribute	
sink		behalf	
behalf		dump	
genius		glance	
glance		device	
specialize		compare	

외우는 게 지루하면 바로 다음 페이지로 넘어가세요!

conceive [kənsíːv]	생각하다, 임신하다
solid [sálid]	고체의, 단단한
ashamed [əʃéimd]	창피한
deposit [dipázit]	예금, 보증금
former [fɔ́ːrmər]	전의, 전임의
suffer [sʌfər]	겪다, 고통을 받다
seek [siːk]	추구하다, 찾다
output [auˈtpʊˌt]	출력, 생산
depress [diprés]	우울하게 만들다
corrupt [kərʌpt]	부패한, 타락한

뜻이 바로 떠오르지 않으면 왼쪽 페이지의 뜻을 보고 적으세요.

conceive		solid	
former		ashamed	
suffer		corrupt	
solid		seek	
seek		depress	
output		conceive	
corrupt		corrupt	
deposit		seek	
ashamed		depress	
depress		former	
conceive		suffer	
suffer		deposit	
seek		solid	
ashamed		ashamed	
deposit		output	
former		conceive	
solid		corrupt	
depress		seek	
output		depress	
corrupt		former	
conceive		suffer	
output		deposit	
former		solid	
seek		ashamed	
depress		output	
corrupt		conceive	
ashamed		former	
suffer		suffer	
solid		solid	
deposit		seek	
conceive		output	
output		corrupt	
suffer		deposit	
deposit		ashamed	
former		depress	

외우는 게 지루하면 바로 다음 페이지로 넘어가세요!

split [split]	분할, 나누다
bounce [bauns]	튀어오르다
insist [insíst]	주장하다
burden [bə́:rdn]	짐, 부담
await [əwéit]	기다리다, 대기하다
yawn [jɔːn]	하품하다
hinder [híndər]	방해하다, 저해하다
propose [prəpóuz]	제안하다, 제시하다
occupy [ákjupài]	점령하다, 차지하다
routine [ruːtíːn]	일상적인, 일과

뜻이 바로 떠오르지 않으면 왼쪽 페이지의 뜻을 보고 적으세요.

split		bounce	
await		insist	
yawn		routine	
bounce		hinder	
hinder		occupy	
propose		split	
routine		routine	
burden		hinder	
insist		occupy	
occupy		await	
split		yawn	
yawn		burden	
hinder		bounce	
insist		insist	
burden		propose	
await		split	
bounce		routine	
occupy		hinder	
propose		occupy	
routine		await	
split		yawn	
propose		burden	
await		bounce	
hinder		insist	
occupy		propose	
routine		split	
insist		await	
yawn		yawn	
bounce		bounce	
burden		hinder	
split		propose	
propose		routine	
yawn		burden	
burden		insist	
await		occupy	

외우는 게 지루하면 바로 다음 페이지로 넘어가세요!

loose [luːs]	느슨해지다, 풀다
resume [rizúːm]	재개하다, 다시 시작하다
spoil [spɔil]	망치다, 상하다
vivid [vívid]	생생한, 발랄한
distort [distɔ́ːrt]	왜곡하다, 뒤틀다
theme [θiːm]	주제, 제목
stir [stəːr]	일으키다
manage [maénidʒ]	관리하다, 운영하다
principle [prínsəpl]	원칙, 원리
bleed [bliːd]	출혈하다

뜻이 바로 떠오르지 않으면 왼쪽 페이지의 뜻을 보고 적으세요.

loose		resume	
distort		spoil	
theme		bleed	
resume		stir	
stir		principle	
manage		loose	
bleed		bleed	
vivid		stir	
spoil		principle	
principle		distort	
loose		theme	
theme		vivid	
stir		resume	
spoil		spoil	
vivid		manage	
distort		loose	
resume		bleed	
principle		stir	
manage		principle	
bleed		distort	
loose		theme	
manage		vivid	
distort		resume	
stir		spoil	
principle		manage	
bleed		loose	
spoil		distort	
themc		theme	
resume		resume	
vivid		stir	
loose		manage	
manage		bleed	
theme		vivid	
vivid		spoil	
distort		principle	

외우는 게 지루하면 바로 다음 페이지로 넘어가세요!

policy [páləsi]	정책, 제도
sequence [síːkwəns]	서열, 순서
actual [ǽktʃuəl]	실제의, 사실상의
glow [glou]	빛나다, 불이 켜지다
shallow [ʃǽlou]	얕은, 얄팍한
wicked [wíkid]	사악한, 부도덕한
affair [əféər]	사건, 문제
union [júːnjən]	노동조합, 단체
circumstance [sə́ːrkəmstæns]	상황, 환경
pursue [pərsúː]	추구하다, 추진하다

뜻이 바로 떠오르지 않으면 왼쪽 페이지의 뜻을 보고 적으세요.

policy		sequence	
shallow		actual	
wicked		pursue	
sequence		affair	
affair		circumstance	
union		policy	
pursue		pursue	
glow		affair	
actual		circumstance	
circumstance		shallow	
policy		wicked	
wicked		glow	
affair		sequence	
actual		actual	
glow		union	
shallow		policy	
sequence		pursue	
circumstance		affair	
union		circumstance	
pursue		shallow	
policy		wicked	
union		glow	
shallow		sequence	
affair		actual	
circumstance		union	
pursue		policy	
actual		shallow	
wicked		wicked	
sequence		sequence	
glow		affair	
policy		union	
union		pursue	
wicked		glow	
glow		actual	
shallow		circumstance	

외우는 게 지루하면 바로 다음 페이지로 넘어가세요!

invade [invéid]	침략하다, 침공
rest [rest]	휴식, 쉬다
fare [fɛər]	운임, 요금
disgrace [disgréis]	불명예
suggest [səgdʒést]	제안하다, 시사하다
treasure [tréʒər]	보물, 소중히 하다
precise [prisáis]	정밀한, 정확한
swallow [swálou]	삼키다, 감수하다
possess [pəzés]	보유하다, 가지다
approve [əprúːv]	승인하다, 허가하다

invade		rest	
suggest		fare	
treasure		approve	
rest		precise	
precise		possess	
swallow		invade	
approve		approve	
disgrace		precise	
fare		possess	
possess		suggest	
invade		treasure	
treasure		disgrace	
precise		rest	
fare		fare	
disgrace		swallow	
suggest		invade	
rest		approve	
possess		precise	
swallow		possess	
approve		suggest	
invade		treasure	
swallow		disgrace	
suggest		rest	
precise		fare	
possess		swallow	
approve		invade	
fare		suggest	
treasure		treasure	
rest		rest	
disgrace		precise	
invade		swallow	
swallow		approve	
treasure		disgrace	
disgrace		fare	
suggest		possess	

외우는 게 지루하면 바로 다음 페이지로 넘어가세요!

execute [éksikjùːt]	처형하다, 집행하다
shave [ʃeiv]	면도하다, 깎다
welfare [wélfɛər]	복지, 후생
murder [mə́ːrdər]	살인, 살해
fame [feim]	명성, 명예
applaud [əplɔ́ːd]	박수 치다, 칭찬하다
forehead [fɔ́ːrid]	이마
accept [æksépt]	받아들이다, 수용하다
psychology [saikálədʒi]	심리
purpose [pə́ːrpəs]	목적, 목표

뜻이 바로 떠오르지 않으면 왼쪽 페이지의 뜻을 보고 적으세요.

execute		shave	
fame		welfare	
applaud		purpose	
shave		forehead	
forehead		psychology	
accept		execute	
purpose		purpose	
murder		forehead	
welfare		psychology	
psychology		fame	
execute		applaud	
applaud		murder	
forehead		shave	
welfare		welfare	
murder		accept	
fame		execute	
shave		purpose	
psychology		forehead	
accept		psychology	
purpose		fame	
execute		applaud	
accept		murder	
fame		shave	
forehead		welfare	
psychology		accept	
purpose		execute	
welfare		fame	
applaud		applaud	
shave		shave	
murder		forehead	
execute		accept	
accept		purpose	
applaud		murder	
murder		welfare	
fame		psychology	

외우는 게 지루하면 바로 다음 페이지로 넘어가세요!

alien [éiljən]	외계인, 외국인
portrait [pɔ́:rtrit]	초상화, 사진
dispose [dispóuz]	배치하다
devote [divóut]	헌신하다, 바치다
conscious [kánʃəs]	의식하는
proper [prápər]	적절한, 제대로
grant [grænt]	부여하다, 주다
climate [kláimit]	기후, 풍토
reserve [rizə́:rv]	보류하다
satisfy [saétisfài]	만족시키다, 충족시키다

뜻이 바로 떠오르지 않으면 왼쪽 페이지의 뜻을 보고 적으세요.

alien	_____	portrait	_____
conscious	_____	dispose	_____
proper	_____	satisfy	_____
portrait	_____	grant	_____
grant	_____	reserve	_____
climate	_____	alien	_____
satisfy	_____	satisfy	_____
devote	_____	grant	_____
dispose	_____	reserve	_____
reserve	_____	conscious	_____
alien	_____	proper	_____
proper	_____	devote	_____
grant	_____	portrait	_____
dispose	_____	dispose	_____
devote	_____	climate	_____
conscious	_____	alien	_____
portrait	_____	satisfy	_____
reserve	_____	grant	_____
climate	_____	reserve	_____
satisfy	_____	conscious	_____
alien	_____	proper	_____
climate	_____	devote	_____
conscious	_____	portrait	_____
grant	_____	dispose	_____
reserve	_____	climate	_____
satisfy	_____	alien	_____
dispose	_____	conscious	_____
proper	_____	proper	_____
portrait	_____	portrait	_____
devote	_____	grant	_____
alien	_____	climate	_____
climate	_____	satisfy	_____
proper	_____	devote	_____
devote	_____	dispose	_____
conscious	_____	reserve	_____

외우는 게 지루하면 바로 다음 페이지로 넘어가세요!

ascribe [əskráib]	~ 탓으로 돌리다.
disorder [disɔ́:rdər]	장애, 질환
cancer [kaénsər]	암, 악성 종양
silly [síli]	어리석은, 바보
chew [tʃuː]	~을 씹다
extract [ikstraékt]	추출하다, 이끌어 내다
resource [ríːsɔːrs]	자원, 부
cathedral [kəθíːdrəl]	대성당
estimate [éstəmèit]	추정하다, 예상하다
survive [sərváiv]	살아남다, 생존하다

뜻이 바로 떠오르지 않으면 왼쪽 페이지의 뜻을 보고 적으세요.

ascribe		disorder	
chew		cancer	
extract		survive	
disorder		resource	
resource		estimate	
cathedral		ascribe	
survive		survive	
silly		resource	
cancer		estimate	
estimate		chew	
ascribe		extract	
extract		silly	
resource		disorder	
cancer		cancer	
silly		cathedral	
chew		ascribe	
disorder		survive	
estimate		resource	
cathedral		estimate	
survive		chew	
ascribe		extract	
cathedral		silly	
chew		disorder	
resource		cancer	
estimate		cathedral	
survive		ascribe	
cancer		chew	
extract		extract	
disorder		disorder	
silly		resource	
ascribe		cathedral	
cathedral		survive	
extract		silly	
silly		cancer	
chew		estimate	

halt [hɔːlt]	중단, 멈추다
comprehend [kámprihénd]	이해하다, 의식하다
labor [léibər]	노동, 근로
practice [praéktis]	관습, 연습하다
proportion [prəpɔ́ːrʃən]	비율, 비례
passive [paésiv]	수동적인, 소극적인
myth [miθ]	신화, 미신
resolve [rizálv]	해결하다, 결의하다
desire [dizáiər]	욕망, 원하다
ecstasy [ékstəsi]	황홀, 황홀경

뜻이 바로 떠오르지 않으면 왼쪽 페이지의 뜻을 보고 적으세요.

halt		comprehend	
proportion		labor	
passive		ecstasy	
comprehend		myth	
myth		desire	
resolve		halt	
ecstasy		ecstasy	
practice		myth	
labor		desire	
desire		proportion	
halt		passive	
passive		practice	
myth		comprehend	
labor		labor	
practice		resolve	
proportion		halt	
comprehend		ecstasy	
desire		myth	
resolve		desire	
ecstasy		proportion	
halt		passive	
resolve		practice	
proportion		comprehend	
myth		labor	
desire		resolve	
ecstasy		halt	
labor		proportion	
passive		passive	
comprehend		comprehend	
practice		myth	
halt		resolve	
resolve		ecstasy	
passive		practice	
practice		labor	
proportion		desire	

외우는 게 지루하면 바로 다음 페이지로 넘어가세요!

spare [spɛər]	아끼다, 남은
evidence [évədəns]	증거, 근거
foretell [fɔrteˈl]	예견하다
delicate [délikət]	섬세한, 민감한
tremble [trémbl]	떨다, 진동하다
rely [rilái]	의존하다, 의지하다
increase [inkríːs]	증가하다, 늘리다
disabled [diséibld]	장애를 가진
religion [rilídʒən]	종교, 신앙
terrify [térəfài]	겁나게 하다, 가혹한

뜻이 바로 떠오르지 않으면 왼쪽 페이지의 뜻을 보고 적으세요.

spare		evidence	
tremble		foretell	
rely		terrify	
evidence		increase	
increase		religion	
disabled		spare	
terrify		terrify	
delicate		increase	
foretell		religion	
religion		tremble	
spare		rely	
rely		delicate	
increase		evidence	
foretell		foretell	
delicate		disabled	
tremble		spare	
evidence		terrify	
religion		increase	
disabled		religion	
terrify		tremble	
spare		rely	
disabled		delicate	
tremble		evidence	
increase		foretell	
religion		disabled	
terrify		spare	
foretell		tremble	
rely		rely	
evidence		evidence	
delicate		increase	
spare		disabled	
disabled		terrify	
rely		delicate	
delicate		foretell	
tremble		religion	

외우는 게 지루하면 바로 다음 페이지로 넘어가세요!

disagree [dìsəgríː]	동의하지 않다, 다르다
memorial [məmɔ́ːriəl]	기념의, 기념관
deal [diːl]	다루다, 거래
destiny [déstəni]	운명, 숙명
capable [kéipəbl]	가능성 있는, 능력 있는
sensation [senséiʃən]	감각, 느낌
barrier [baériər]	장벽, 장애물
wound [wuːnd]	상처, 고통
administer [ədmínistər]	관리하다, 투여하다
reputation [rèpjutéiʃən]	명성, 평판

뜻이 바로 떠오르지 않으면 왼쪽 페이지의 뜻을 보고 적으세요.

disagree		memorial	
capable		deal	
sensation		reputation	
memorial		barrier	
barrier		administer	
wound		disagree	
reputation		reputation	
destiny		barrier	
deal		administer	
administer		capable	
disagree		sensation	
sensation		destiny	
barrier		memorial	
deal		deal	
destiny		wound	
capable		disagree	
memorial		reputation	
administer		barrier	
wound		administer	
reputation		capable	
disagree		sensation	
wound		destiny	
capable		memorial	
barrier		deal	
administer		wound	
reputation		disagree	
deal		capable	
sensation		sensation	
memorial		memorial	
destiny		barrier	
disagree		wound	
wound		reputation	
sensation		destiny	
destiny		deal	
capable		administer	

외우는 게 지루하면 바로 다음 페이지로 넘어가세요!

bald [bɔːld]	대머리의
context [kántekst]	문맥, 상황
literary [lítərèri]	문학, 작품
compose [kəmpóuz]	구성하다, 작곡하다
commit [kəmít]	저지르다, 범하다
feed [fiːd]	공급하다, 먹이, 사료
pulse [pʌls]	맥박, 파동
arrow [aérou]	화살
odd [ad]	이상한, 특이한
recycle [riːsáikl]	재활용하다, 재생하다

뜻이 바로 떠오르지 않으면 왼쪽 페이지의 뜻을 보고 적으세요.

bald		context	
commit		literary	
feed		recycle	
context		pulse	
pulse		odd	
arrow		bald	
recycle		recycle	
compose		pulse	
literary		odd	
odd		commit	
bald		feed	
feed		compose	
pulse		context	
literary		literary	
compose		arrow	
commit		bald	
context		recycle	
odd		pulse	
arrow		odd	
recycle		commit	
bald		feed	
arrow		compose	
commit		context	
pulse		literary	
odd		arrow	
recycle		bald	
literary		commit	
feed		feed	
context		context	
compose		pulse	
bald		arrow	
arrow		recycle	
feed		compose	
compose		literary	
commit		odd	

외우는 게 지루하면 바로 다음 페이지로 넘어가세요!

retreat [ritríːt]	후퇴, 물러서다
emphasize [émfəsàiz]	강조하다
trim [trim]	잘라 내다, 다듬다
flaw [flɔː]	결점, 흠
eliminate [ilímənèit]	없애다, 제거하다
wander [wándər]	돌아다니다, 배회하다
terrible [térəbl]	끔찍한, 무서운
passion [páéʃən]	열정, 흥미
noble [nóubl]	고귀한, 귀족의
attach [ətáétʃ]	포함하다, 부착하다

뜻이 바로 떠오르지 않으면 왼쪽 페이지의 뜻을 보고 적으세요.

retreat		emphasize	
eliminate		trim	
wander		attach	
emphasize		terrible	
terrible		noble	
passion		retreat	
attach		attach	
flaw		terrible	
trim		noble	
noble		eliminate	
retreat		wander	
wander		flaw	
terrible		emphasize	
trim		trim	
flaw		passion	
eliminate		retreat	
emphasize		attach	
noble		terrible	
passion		noble	
attach		eliminate	
retreat		wander	
passion		flaw	
eliminate		emphasize	
terrible		trim	
noble		passion	
attach		retreat	
trim		eliminate	
wander		wander	
emphasize		emphasize	
flaw		terrible	
retreat		passion	
passion		attach	
wander		flaw	
flaw		trim	
eliminate		noble	

외우는 게 지루하면 바로 다음 페이지로 넘어가세요!

erupt [irʌpt]	폭발하다, 발생하다
verse [vəːrs]	시, 노래
occur [əkə́ːr]	발생하다, 일어나다
exhibit [igzíbit]	전시, 전시회
harvest [háːrvist]	수확, 추수
scrub [skrʌb]	문지르다, 닦다
pile [pail]	쌓다, 모으다
employ [implɔ́i]	고용하다
embrace [imbréis]	포용하다, 받아들이다
canal [kənaél]	운하

뜻이 바로 떠오르지 않으면 왼쪽 페이지의 뜻을 보고 적으세요.

erupt		verse	
harvest		occur	
scrub		canal	
verse		pile	
pile		embrace	
employ		erupt	
canal		canal	
exhibit		pile	
occur		embrace	
embrace		harvest	
erupt		scrub	
scrub		exhibit	
pile		verse	
occur		occur	
exhibit		employ	
harvest		erupt	
verse		canal	
embrace		pile	
employ		embrace	
canal		harvest	
erupt		scrub	
employ		exhibit	
harvest		verse	
pile		occur	
embrace		employ	
canal		erupt	
occur		harvest	
scrub		scrub	
verse		verse	
exhibit		pile	
erupt		employ	
employ		canal	
scrub		exhibit	
exhibit		occur	
harvest		embrace	

외우는 게 지루하면 바로 다음 페이지로 넘어가세요!

surpass [sərpaés]	넘어서다, 앞서다
announce [ənáuns]	발표하다, 밝히다
asset [aéset]	자산, 재산
summit [sʌ́mit]	최고봉, 정상
biography [baiágrəfi]	자서전, 전기
destination [dèstənéiʃən]	목적지, 관광지
merit [mérit]	장점, 이점
object [ábdʒikt]	물건, 객체
recognize [rékəgnàiz]	인정하다, 인식하다
sphere [sfiər]	구, 구체, 영역

뜻이 바로 떠오르지 않으면 왼쪽 페이지의 뜻을 보고 적으세요.

surpass		announce	
biography		asset	
destination		sphere	
announce		merit	
merit		recognize	
object		surpass	
sphere		sphere	
summit		merit	
asset		recognize	
recognize		biography	
surpass		destination	
destination		summit	
merit		announce	
asset		asset	
summit		object	
biography		surpass	
announce		sphere	
recognize		merit	
object		recognize	
sphere		biography	
surpass		destination	
object		summit	
biography		announce	
merit		asset	
recognize		object	
sphere		surpass	
asset		biography	
destination		destination	
announce		announce	
summit		merit	
surpass		object	
object		sphere	
destination		summit	
summit		asset	
biography		recognize	

외우는 게 지루하면 바로 다음 페이지로 넘어가세요!

persevere [pə̀ːrsəvíər]	인내하다, 이겨 내다
ambition [æmbíʃən]	야망, 야심
capacity [kəpaésəti]	능력, 용량
install [instɔ́ːl]	설치하다, 장착하다
opponent [əpóunənt]	반대의, 상대
nod [nad]	끄덕이다, 목례하다
tide [taid]	밀물과 썰물
timber [tímbər]	목재
aware [əwéər]	알고 있는, 인식하는
punctual [pʌ́ŋktʃuəl]	시간을 잘 지키는

뜻이 바로 떠오르지 않으면 왼쪽 페이지의 뜻을 보고 적으세요.

persevere		ambition	
opponent		capacity	
nod		punctual	
ambition		tide	
tide		aware	
timber		persevere	
punctual		punctual	
install		tide	
capacity		aware	
aware		opponent	
persevere		nod	
nod		install	
tide		ambition	
capacity		capacity	
install		timber	
opponent		persevere	
ambition		punctual	
aware		tide	
timber		aware	
punctual		opponent	
persevere		nod	
timber		install	
opponent		ambition	
tide		capacity	
aware		timber	
punctual		persevere	
capacity		opponent	
nod		nod	
ambition		ambition	
install		tide	
persevere		timber	
timber		punctual	
nod		install	
install		capacity	
opponent		aware	

mob [mab]	폭도, 집단
secure [sikjúər]	보장하다, 안전한
issue [íʃuː]	문제, 쟁점
reign [rein]	통치하다, 재임하다
depend [dipénd]	의존하다
primitive [prímətiv]	원시의, 원초적인
effort [éfərt]	노력, 작업
masterpiece [mæˈstərpiˌs]	걸작, 명작
spectacle [spéktəkl]	장관, 광경
poison [pɔ́izn]	독, 중독되다

뜻이 바로 떠오르지 않으면 왼쪽 페이지의 뜻을 보고 적으세요.

mob		secure	
depend		issue	
primitive		poison	
secure		effort	
effort		spectacle	
masterpiece		mob	
poison		poison	
reign		effort	
issue		spectacle	
spectacle		depend	
mob		primitive	
primitive		reign	
effort		secure	
issue		issue	
reign		masterpiece	
depend		mob	
secure		poison	
spectacle		effort	
masterpiece		spectacle	
poison		depend	
mob		primitive	
masterpiece		reign	
depend		secure	
effort		issue	
spectacle		masterpiece	
poison		mob	
issue		depend	
primitive		primitive	
secure		secure	
reign		effort	
mob		masterpiece	
masterpiece		poison	
primitive		reign	
reign		issue	
depend		spectacle	

외우는 게 지루하면 바로 다음 페이지로 넘어가세요!

constant [kánstənt]	일정한, 지속적인
retain [ritéin]	유지하다, 보유하다
expense [ikspéns]	비용, 지출
pat [pæt]	쓰다듬다, 두드리다
concrete [kánkri:t]	구체적인, 확실한
bother [báðər]	괴롭히다, 성가시게 하다
dull [dʌl]	지루한, 따분한
impact [ímpækt]	영향, 충격
mixture [míkstʃər]	혼합, 섞인
squeeze [skwi:z]	압착하다, 짜내다

constant		retain	
concrete		expense	
bother		squeeze	
retain		dull	
dull		mixture	
impact		constant	
squeeze		squeeze	
pat		dull	
expense		mixture	
mixture		concrete	
constant		bother	
bother		pat	
dull		retain	
expense		expense	
pat		impact	
concrete		constant	
retain		squeeze	
mixture		dull	
impact		mixture	
squeeze		concrete	
constant		bother	
impact		pat	
concrete		retain	
dull		expense	
mixture		impact	
squeeze		constant	
expense		concrete	
bother		bother	
retain		retain	
pat		dull	
constant		impact	
impact		squeeze	
bother		pat	
pat		expense	
concrete		mixture	

외우는 게 지루하면 바로 다음 페이지로 넘어가세요!

equipment [ikwípmənt]	장비, 기기
fluent [flúːənt]	유창한, 능통한
despise [dispáiz]	경멸하다, 멸시하다
extend [iksténd]	확장하다, 연장하다
situation [sìtʃuéiʃən]	상황, 사태
tough [tʌf]	힘든, 어려운
pity [píti]	동정, 연민, 유감
pioneer [pàiəníər]	개척자, 개척하다
struggle [strʌgl]	투쟁하다, 분투하다
draft [dræft]	초안, 입안

뜻이 바로 떠오르지 않으면 왼쪽 페이지의 뜻을 보고 적으세요.

equipment		fluent	
situation		despise	
tough		draft	
fluent		pity	
pity		struggle	
pioneer		equipment	
draft		draft	
extend		pity	
despise		struggle	
struggle		situation	
equipment		tough	
tough		extend	
pity		fluent	
despise		despise	
extend		pioneer	
situation		equipment	
fluent		draft	
struggle		pity	
pioneer		struggle	
draft		situation	
equipment		tough	
pioneer		extend	
situation		fluent	
pity		despise	
struggle		pioneer	
draft		equipment	
despise		situation	
tough		tough	
fluent		fluent	
extend		pity	
equipment		pioneer	
pioneer		draft	
tough		extend	
extend		despise	
situation		struggle	

retail [ríːteil]	소매, 유통
forgive [fərgív]	용서하다, 양해하다
irritate [írətèit]	짜증 나게 하다
stubborn [stʌ́bərn]	고집 센, 완고한
leisure [líːʒər]	여가, 한가한
treat [triːt]	치료하다, 대하다
victim [víktim]	피해자, 희생자
investigate [invéstəgèit]	조사하다, 수사하다
utilize [júːtəlàiz]	활용하다, 이용하다
geometry [dʒiámətri]	기하학

뜻이 바로 떠오르지 않으면 왼쪽 페이지의 뜻을 보고 적으세요.

retail		forgive	
leisure		irritate	
treat		geometry	
forgive		victim	
victim		utilize	
investigate		retail	
geometry		geometry	
stubborn		victim	
irritate		utilize	
utilize		leisure	
retail		treat	
treat		stubborn	
victim		forgive	
irritate		irritate	
stubborn		investigate	
leisure		retail	
forgive		geometry	
utilize		victim	
investigate		utilize	
geometry		leisure	
retail		treat	
investigate		stubborn	
leisure		forgive	
victim		irritate	
utilize		investigate	
geometry		retail	
irritate		leisure	
treat		treat	
forgive		forgive	
stubborn		victim	
retail		investigate	
investigate		geometry	
treat		stubborn	
stubborn		irritate	
leisure		utilize	

외우는 게 지루하면 바로 다음 페이지로 넘어가세요!

defend [difénd]	방어하다, 지키다
attribute [ətríbjuːt]	~로 여기다
source [sɔːrs]	원천
intense [inténs]	강렬한, 심한
modest [mάdist]	겸손한, 적당한
treaty [tríːti]	조약, 협정
terrific [tərífik]	대단한, 무서운
accord [əkɔ́ːrd]	협정, 합의
virtue [və́ːrtʃuː]	미덕, 덕목
ban [bæn]	금지, 규제

defend		attribute	
modest		source	
treaty		ban	
attribute		terrific	
terrific		virtue	
accord		defend	
ban		ban	
intense		terrific	
source		virtue	
virtue		modest	
defend		treaty	
treaty		intense	
terrific		attribute	
source		source	
intense		accord	
modest		defend	
attribute		ban	
virtue		terrific	
accord		virtue	
ban		modest	
defend		treaty	
accord		intense	
modest		attribute	
terrific		source	
virtue		accord	
ban		defend	
source		modest	
treaty		treaty	
attribute		attribute	
intense		terrific	
defend		accord	
accord		ban	
treaty		intense	
intense		source	
modest		virtue	

외우는 게 지루하면 바로 다음 페이지로 넘어가세요!

contract [kənˈtrækt]	계약서, 계약
bare [bɛər]	노출된, 드러내다
generous [dʒénərəs]	관대한, 후한
therapy [θérəpi]	치료, 요법
inferior [infíəriər]	열등한
complex [kəmplék]	복잡한, 복합의
senior [síːnjər]	선임, 고령자
minister [mínəstər]	장관, 목사
entertain [èntərtéin]	즐겁게 하다, 접대하다
gorgeous [góːrdʒəs]	멋진, 우아한

뜻이 바로 떠오르지 않으면 왼쪽 페이지의 뜻을 보고 적으세요.

contract		bare	
inferior		generous	
complex		gorgeous	
bare		senior	
senior		entertain	
minister		contract	
gorgeous		gorgeous	
therapy		senior	
generous		entertain	
entertain		inferior	
contract		complex	
complex		therapy	
senior		bare	
generous		generous	
therapy		minister	
inferior		contract	
bare		gorgeous	
entertain		senior	
minister		entertain	
gorgeous		inferior	
contract		complex	
minister		therapy	
inferior		bare	
senior		generous	
entertain		minister	
gorgeous		contract	
generous		inferior	
complex		complex	
bare		bare	
therapy		senior	
contract		minister	
minister		gorgeous	
complex		therapy	
therapy		generous	
inferior		entertain	

외우는 게 지루하면 바로 다음 페이지로 넘어가세요!

architecture [á:rkɪtèktʃər]	건축, 설계
wipe [waip]	닦다, 없애다
interfere [ìntərfíər]	간섭하다, 방해하다
circulate [sə́:rkjulèit]	돌다, 유통되다
support [səpɔ́:rt]	지원하다, 지지하다
rent [rent]	임대하다, 빌리다
process [práses]	과정, 공정
emit [imít]	방출하다, 내뿜다
decade [dékeid]	10년간, 수십 년
expedition [èkspədíʃən]	탐험, 여행

뜻이 바로 떠오르지 않으면 왼쪽 페이지의 뜻을 보고 적으세요.

architecture		wipe	
support		interfere	
rent		expedition	
wipe		process	
process		decade	
emit		architecture	
expedition		expedition	
circulate		process	
interfere		decade	
decade		support	
architecture		rent	
rent		circulate	
process		wipe	
interfere		interfere	
circulate		emit	
support		architecture	
wipe		expedition	
decade		process	
emit		decade	
expedition		support	
architecture		rent	
emit		circulate	
support		wipe	
process		interfere	
decade		emit	
expedition		architecture	
interfere		support	
rent		rent	
wipe		wipe	
circulate		process	
architecture		emit	
emit		expedition	
rent		circulate	
circulate		interfere	
support		decade	

외우는 게 지루하면 바로 다음 페이지로 넘어가세요!

term [təːrm]	임기, 용어
contrary [kántreri]	반대의, 정반대의
pretend [priténd]	~ 척하다, 가장하다
revive [riváiv]	소생시키다, 되살아나다
loan [loun]	대출, 빌려주다
ash [æʃ]	재, 화산재
frustrate [frʌstreit]	좌절시키다
heal [hiːl]	치유되다, 치료하다
scent [sent]	향기, 냄새
rod [rab]	막대기

뜻이 바로 떠오르지 않으면 왼쪽 페이지의 뜻을 보고 적으세요.

term	_____	contrary	_____
loan	_____	pretend	_____
ash	_____	rod	_____
contrary	_____	frustrate	_____
frustrate	_____	scent	_____
heal	_____	term	_____
rod	_____	rod	_____
revive	_____	frustrate	_____
pretend	_____	scent	_____
scent	_____	loan	_____
term	_____	ash	_____
ash	_____	revive	_____
frustrate	_____	contrary	_____
pretend	_____	pretend	_____
revive	_____	heal	_____
loan	_____	term	_____
contrary	_____	rod	_____
scent	_____	frustrate	_____
heal	_____	scent	_____
rod	_____	loan	_____
term	_____	ash	_____
heal	_____	revive	_____
loan	_____	contrary	_____
frustrate	_____	pretend	_____
scent	_____	heal	_____
rod	_____	term	_____
pretend	_____	loan	_____
ash	_____	ash	_____
contrary	_____	contrary	_____
revive	_____	frustrate	_____
term	_____	heal	_____
heal	_____	rod	_____
ash	_____	revive	_____
revive	_____	pretend	_____
loan	_____	scent	_____

외우는 게 지루하면 바로 다음 페이지로 넘어가세요!

tremendous [triméndəs]	엄청난, 대단한
bend [bend]	구부러지다
genuine [dʒénjuin]	진실된, 진짜의
splash [splæʃ]	끼얹다
violate [váiəlèit]	위반하다, 침해하다
compile [kəmpáil]	편집하다, 수집하다
weird [wiərd]	이상한, 기묘한
yield [jiːld]	산출하다, 생산하다
impulse [ímpʌls]	충동, 자극
abuse [əbjúːz]	학대하다, 남용하다

tremendous		bend	
violate		genuine	
compile		abuse	
bend		weird	
weird		impulse	
yield		tremendous	
abuse		abuse	
splash		weird	
genuine		impulse	
impulse		violate	
tremendous		compile	
compile		splash	
weird		bend	
genuine		genuine	
splash		yield	
violate		tremendous	
bend		abuse	
impulse		weird	
yield		impulse	
abuse		violate	
tremendous		compile	
yield		splash	
violate		bend	
weird		genuine	
impulse		yield	
abuse		tremendous	
genuine		violate	
compile		compile	
bend		bend	
splash		weird	
tremendous		yield	
yield		abuse	
compile		splash	
splash		genuine	
violate		impulse	

외우는 게 지루하면 바로 다음 페이지로 넘어가세요!

decay [dikéi]	부패, 붕괴하다
kneel [ni:l]	무릎을 꿇다, 굴복하다
preserve [prizə́:rv]	보존하다, 보호하다
exact [igzaékt]	정확한, 완전한
native [néitiv]	원주민의, 토착의
brilliant [bríljənt]	훌륭한, 뛰어난
frost [frɔ:st]	얼어붙다, 결빙
instruct [instrʌ́kt]	지시하다, 알려 주다
thrift [θrift]	절약, 검소
rural [rúərəl]	농업의, 시골의

decay		kneel	
native		preserve	
brilliant		rural	
kneel		frost	
frost		thrift	
instruct		decay	
rural		rural	
exact		frost	
preserve		thrift	
thrift		native	
decay		brilliant	
brilliant		exact	
frost		kneel	
preserve		preserve	
exact		instruct	
native		decay	
kneel		rural	
thrift		frost	
instruct		thrift	
rural		native	
decay		brilliant	
instruct		exact	
native		kneel	
frost		preserve	
thrift		instruct	
rural		decay	
preserve		native	
brilliant		brilliant	
kneel		kneel	
exact		frost	
decay		instruct	
instruct		rural	
brilliant		exact	
exact		preserve	
native		thrift	

외우는 게 지루하면 바로 다음 페이지로 넘어가세요!

hire [haiər]	고용하다, 채용하다
insure [inʃúər]	보장하다, 보험에 들다
beam [biːm]	광선
perish [périʃ]	사라지다, 죽다
transplant [trænsplæ'nt]	이식하다, 이식
grasp [græsp]	이해하다, 잡다
drag [dræg]	끌어내다, 장애물
detach [ditaétʃ]	단독의, 분리하다
acquire [əkwáiər]	얻다, 인수하다
famine [faémin]	기근, 기아, 굶주림

뜻이 바로 떠오르지 않으면 왼쪽 페이지의 뜻을 보고 적으세요.

hire		insure	
transplant		beam	
grasp		famine	
insure		drag	
drag		acquire	
detach		hire	
famine		famine	
perish		drag	
beam		acquire	
acquire		transplant	
hire		grasp	
grasp		perish	
drag		insure	
beam		beam	
perish		detach	
transplant		hire	
insure		famine	
acquire		drag	
detach		acquire	
famine		transplant	
hire		grasp	
detach		perish	
transplant		insure	
drag		beam	
acquire		detach	
famine		hire	
beam		transplant	
grasp		grasp	
insure		insure	
perish		drag	
hire		detach	
detach		famine	
grasp		perish	
perish		beam	
transplant		acquire